Conservative Mythology and Public Policy in America

Conservative Mythology and Public Policy in America

ARNOLD VEDLITZ

New York
Westport, Connecticut
London

Library of Congress Cataloging-in-Publication Data

Vedlitz, Arnold.
   Conservative mythology and public policy in
America.

   Bibliography: p.
   Includes index.
   1. Conservatism—United States. 2. United States—
Politics and government—1981–   . 3. United States—
Economic policy—1981–   . 4. United States—Social
policy—1980–   . I. Title.
JA84.U5V43   1988   320.5′2′0973   88-17961
   ISBN 0-275-92641-9 (alk. paper)

Library of Congress Catalog Card Number: 88–17961
ISBN: 0–275–92641–9

First published in 1988

Praeger Publishers, One Madison Avenue, New York, NY 10010
A division of Greenwood Press, Inc.

Printed in the United States of America

∞

The paper used in this book complies with the
Permanent Paper Standard issued by the National
Information Standards Organization (Z39.48–1984).

10 9 8 7 6 5 4 3 2 1

To

Rose Vedlitz and Abbie Jackson

Contents

Illustrations

TABLES

FIGURES

Conservative Mythology and Public Policy in America

1

Myths and Politics in America

The U.S. political system is a complicated one. It is filled with overlapping and competing structures and institutions, and citizens find themselves in a maze of local, state, and national rules, regulations, obligations, and opportunities. In this complex system, however, the citizen is more than a passive victim of governmental caprice; more than a passive recipient of government largesse. The citizen is, in many ways, at the heart of the political system. In our own ways, each of us helps control the governmental structures and policies that both frustrate and serve us.

We exercise this control because collectively we act as approvers, guiders, and limiters of what our various governments do. This collective action is exercised directly through political actions, such as voting, political-party activity, and political-interest-group activity. More important, this control is exerted indirectly by our consensus on political values, our shared acceptance or rejection of the appropriateness of particular governmental actions. Our beliefs and attitudes about the rightness or wrongness of governmental policies place profound limits on our political decision makers. This shared set of political beliefs, which we refer to as "consensus," provides directions and limits that politicians ignore at great peril to their careers. The political graveyards are full of politicians who were too far ahead of or too far behind the consensual center of their constituencies.

Our consensus goes beyond simple agreement on political forms and contemporary public-policy directions. It encompasses fundamental societal symbols and myths that underlie our sense of who we are, how we got here, where we should go, and what we owe our fellow citizens. Each society has a central core of beliefs that provides it with a collective psychological center. Anthropologists call this central core the society's world view or ethos, and they stress its importance in maintaining societal stability and direction and in providing the subtle and not so subtle differences that distinguish one society from another. R. M. MacIver, in his classic treatise *The Web of Government,* has expressed this position better than most:

Every civilization, every period, every nation, has its characteristic myth-complex. In it lies the secret of social unities and every society. Wherever he goes, whatever he encounters, man spins about him his web of myth, as the caterpillar spins its cocoon. Every individual spins his own variant within the greater web of the whole group. The myth mediates between man and nature. From the shelter of his myth he perceives and experiences the world. Inside his myth he is at home in his world.[1]

Nation-states are the major institutional arrangement within which large and complex societies exist. Recent events have shown us that MacIver's proposition may not be equally true for all nation-states. Because nations are often artificially created entities, not always evolving naturally out of a common society or culture, they may hold within them a number of different subculture groups. These smaller groupings may or may not be bound by fundamental common values. Frequently, the greatest task of nation building is welding together these numerous, often competing factions into a single, coherent culture group. As the news reports of continuing violence coming to us daily from such nations as Northern Ireland and Lebanon make all too clear, many nations have not successfully created an overarching set of cultural beliefs and identities that unite their peoples.

Scholars who have examined internal national conflicts acknowledge that all nations have cleavages, divisions that separate citizens into unique groups that hold different views and support different government policies.[2] These scholars have identified two types of cleavages found in different degrees in different countries. The presence of one type of cleavage rather than the other has a tremendous impact on a nation's stability and unity.

The first and most benign set of cleavages is referred to as "cross-cutting," a condition in which various groups are arrayed against one another on various issues. For example, let us assume that Nation X contains four identifiable groups: the blues, the greens, the blacks, and the whites. Under conditions of cross-cutting cleavages, the blues and greens may be arrayed against the blacks and whites on issue #1. On issue #2, it is the blacks and greens who are arrayed against the blues and whites. And on issue #3, it is the greens and whites who are arrayed against the blues and blacks. The result of such divisions is that no one group or set of groups is forever at odds with the others. They may disagree on some issues and agree on others. No group is always the winner and no group is always the loser. Such a system provides the opening for groups to disagree peacefully on important issues, while holding a wide consensus on basis cultural values.

The second and more problematic set of cleavages is referred to as "reinforcing." Under conditions of reinforcing cleavages, the blues and greens in Nation X may always be arrayed against the blacks and whites, regardless of the issue. Whenever there is a fundamental disagreement on social, economic, religious, or political matters in Nation X, it is certain that the blues and greens will be on one side and the blacks and whites on the other. One group or set of groups may always win and another set may always lose. Such cleavages produce bitter conflicts and hostilities and provide no basis on which to build a common, peaceful, supportive, and broad-based cultural identity. We can see the groups within such nations acting out their frustrations, hostility, and bitterness every day. For them, nation building has failed; there is no common, deeply held set of beliefs that can unite these distinct citizen groups.

We are fortunate in the United States in that we more closely fit MacIver's proposition. We have differences, but our cleavages have not prevented us from establishing a central, national cutural center. Individuals and groups do engage in conflict over a number of issues, but it is unusual for one group always to be pitted against another. Groups continuously form and re-form coalitions, depending on the issue currently being discussed. All groups will experience both the blush of success and the gloom of defeat. We can disagree and still share the fundamental values, myths, symbols, and beliefs that weld us as a nation.

This does not mean that our disagreements are insignificant or unimportant. They are real disagreements about important policy questions, and there are definite winners and losers, but these disgreements take place within an overall context of shared basic values. As we discuss and analyze divergent ideologies, disagreements, and policy preferences in the United States, we should keep this fact in mind. Let us look now at this central core around which both our agreements and disagreements revolve. We can distinguish two kinds of politically relevant phenomena that are essential elements of both our shared cultural center and our group differences:

1. Political myths—fundamental beliefs about how the world does or should operate and the proper role of government and the individual within this world;
2. Political symbols—concrete, observable objects, individuals, or institutions that refer to these myths and elicit our feelings about them.

Understanding our myths and symbols will help us to better understand ourselves and the political world we create to govern us.

POLITICAL MYTHS AND SYMBOLS

When we think of myths, two unique concepts come to mind. The first is of powerful, traditional beliefs that rest at the core of a society's culture. This is the concept referred to by MacIver and cultural anthropologists. Such myths include beliefs related to supreme beings, to the origins and purpose of the society, to the role of the individual in society, and to the relationship of the group to its physical environment. The second concept we associate with myth is that of less fundamental beliefs that are held by groups, beliefs that are not necessarily supported by strong empirical evidence. Examples include the myth that Irishmen are strong drinkers, that white southerners are racists, or that California wines are significantly inferior to European ones.

Given the strong differences in the meanings of the word myth, we would expect that few people would get the concepts confused. On most politically relevant issues, however, many of us do have problems distinguishing between basic, traditional beliefs, which I will call primary myths, and more superficial ones, which I will call secondary myths. The problem arises because in the world of political beliefs and values, secondary myths are often derived from the primary myths, with the result that they are difficult to separate from one another. We often invest secondary myths with the positive feelings and reverence that should properly be reserved and invoked only for the more fundamental, primary myths. How does this distinction get blurred?

Historical observer Alexis de Tocqueville, historian Richard Hofstadter, and social critic Walter Lippmann have all suggested that Americans evidence a great deal of agreement on their primary myths.[3] What de Tocqueville calls the philosophical method of the Americans, what Hofstadter calls our American poilitical tradition, and what Lippmann calls our public philosophy are really the same fundamental values, a set of beliefs supporting freedom, equal opportunity, constitutional government, individual participation and responsibility, nationalism, and capitalism. These are broadly constructed concepts, however,—nebulous terms that can be interpreted in different and often conflicting ways.

Various groups in our society, especially those with ideological points of view, find it advantageous to link less basic, more superficial beliefs to fundamental principles of U.S. politics and society. It is then possible to invest these secondary, derivative beliefs with the positive mythical aura of the primary ones. Here is how this happens.

Most Americans—conservatives, moderates, liberals, and even apoliticals—share primary, abstract beliefs in the importance of the set of values articulated by de Tocqueville, Hofstadter, Lippmann, and others. What do these beliefs mean, however, when applied to more specific situations? Take the concept of freedom, for example. Liberals usually believe that freedom can be upheld only by bringing the power of the government into play to protect the rights of the less powerful in society from infringement by those with greater power. In this ideological set, freedoms of one group are protected by restricting or regulating certain actions by others. Conservatives, on the other hand, believe that freedom is best served by letting individuals act within their own abilities and without governmental interference in supporting particular, less fortunate groups. Moderates will fit somewhere in between these two view points.

From the basic myth or value of freedom, then, the liberal myth is that active governmental intervention is needed to protect freedoms, while the conservative myth is that freedom is preserved by preventing the government from interfering in individual actions or exchanges. For liberals, the primary myth of freedom becomes linked to a set of specific governmental programs that intervene to protect certain groups. For conservatives the primary myth of freedom becomes linked to policy preferences that oppose direct government interference in the affairs of citizens.

Disagreements can exist over such issues and values as freedom, since although most of us agree on the primary myths, we can and do disagree on the secondary ones. Because these secondary myths are tied more directly to specific governmental actions and inactions, they often play the greater role in politics.

Political symbols are the concrete referents that evoke the basic positive and negative emotions we have about our fundamental values. Symbols are the building blocks of myth. Such evocative symbols as the Statue of Liberty and the Liberty Bell support our mythical value of freedom for all and equality of opportunity in the United States. Political scientists have discussed the importance of political symbols for the operation of U.S. political systems. Some, such as Murray Edelman,[4] view symbols as manipulative tools used by politicians to get what they want from citizens. Others take the more complex view that symbols can serve both citizens' and politicians' policy goals.[5] Both agree, however, that symbols are powerful evocative tools that call up fundamental beliefs and are key elements we must consider, if we are to understand U.S. politics. Walter Lippmann stressed the importance of symbols in his classic work, *Public Opinion:*

When a coalition around the symbol has been effected, feeling flows toward conformity under the symbol rather than toward critical scrutiny of the measures. . . . He who captures the symbols by which public feeling is for the moment contained, controls by that much the approaches of public policy. And as long as a particular symbol has the power of coalition, ambitious factions will fight for possession. . . . There are limits, of course. Too violent abuse of the actualities which groups of people think the symbol represents, or too great resistance in the name of that symbol to new purposes, will, so to speak, burst the symbol.[6]

As Lippmann implies, myths and symbols are a two-edged sword, which can both serve an interest in one instance and become a barrier in another. An interesting, although sad, example of the positive and negative impacts the manipulation of symbols can have on an issue is President Reagan's 1985 visit to the German military cemetery at Bitburg. One need only review the controversy stirred up by this visit to a military cemetery where 48 Waffen SS troops are buried to see both the compelling importance and the potential dangers of symbol manipulation in the arena of public policy and real-world politics. This particular visit was symbolic on many levels:

1. The president as symbol of the U.S. citizenry

2. The cemetery as symbol of Germany's past participation and guilt associated with World War II

3. The visit to the graves of the enemy as symbol of our forgiveness of the Germans and our desire for reconciliation

4. The visit as a symbol to Jews and to many Allied soldiers of a denial of their past sufferings

5. The reaction to the visit as a symbol that all must remember and know the events that transpired under the Nazis in World War II and that symbolically must never be forgotten or forgiven

6. The desire of the Germans to be forgiven as a symbol of their full acceptance into the Western democratic alliance

7. West German Chancellor Helmut Kohl as a symbol of West Germany

8. Kohl's visit to the concentration camp at Bergen Belsen as a symbol of German recognition of and atonement for Germany's past actions.

It is difficult to keep track of all the symbolic overtones of this set of acts, and it was impossible for either leader, Reagan or Kohl, to avoid having the symbols wrenched from them and used to serve other equally relevant purposes. Much of the symbolism here is contradictory, with different groups reading different meanings into the same actions.

The secondary myths citizens and politicians hold dear, and the symbols they manipulate to move others to share their point of view, are at the core of political conflict in the United States. Understanding such myths and their symbols is essential for sorting out the realities of public policy.

There are hundreds of secondary myths and their supportive symbols operating in the U.S. political arena today. These secondary myths may or may not be based on solid, factual underpinnings. In other words, basic elements of these myths may or may not be true. In many cases, it is impossible to determine empirically the validity of a myth, because it may be based only on wishes and assertions and not subject to validation by factual observation. I present two myths below for illustrative purposes: the myth of the American cowboy and the myth of the nation as especially chosen by God.

The American Cowboy

The myth of the American cowboy is probably one of the best known in the United States. We have seen it played and replayed in movies, television shows, and literature for most of this century.[7] The elements of the myth are relatively consistent: hard-working, hard-drinking, hard-fighting, individualistic white cowboys tame a harsh land, hostile Indians, and corrupt businessmen and politicians. Women play little, if any, active role in the myth of conquering the West. They are usually victims, dupes, or helpless know-nothings, needing guidance from the knowledgable and condescending cowboy/hero. Minorities are also generally absent from our cowboy myth. It would seem from the representations of the cowboy myth in literature and movies that the cowboys and horse soldiers who won the West are singularly white ones. If minorities are present, either Hispanic or black, they appear as relatively insignificant characters, passive bit players rather than active participants in the great western experience.

Cowboy heroes are portrayed as rugged individualists. They neither seek nor need group help or community efforts. More can be accomplished through individual effort. Governments are typically shown to be corrupt, ineffective, inefficient, and foolish, except for the heroic, individualistic cowboy/lawman who overcomes citizen ineptitude or resistance in getting the job done. The myth of the cowboy that has been handed down to us by movies, television shows, and popular western literature can be evaluated by using historical facts to determine the fundamental validity or invalidity of the myth's underlying arguments. As we shall see, the reality is quite different from the myth.

Historians have studied the development of the West in great detail and have chronicled the cowboy's role.[8] The view these scholars present is a more complex one than that asserted by the myth. The cowboy gunslinger was, in fact, a rarity.[9] Government, as represented by the military, was an important protecting and stabilizing force; and group and community efforts were also important. Keeping the peace was usually a community, not an individual, effort, with judges, juries, posses, lawmen, public officials, and concerned citizens all participating. Women also played a direct and vital role in taming the West.[10] They performed farm and ranch work as well as engaging in business and civic activities. After all, most of what civilizes and advances an area is employment/productivity related, not a few violent reactions to real or perceived enemies. Thus, women were important in western economic and social productivity.

The absence of blacks in the myth is equally unfair. There were many black cowboys in the West, and although their numbers were substantially less than those of the whites, they were not insignificant. In some areas they made up a substantial part of the working cowboy population. For example, scholars estimate that blacks accounted for 20–25 percent of those employed in the Texas cattle industry.[11] Even more telling, however, is the contribution blacks made to the western military effort. Black soldiers of the 9th and 10th cavalry and the 24th and 25th infantry regiments were important players in the Indian wars that made the western frontier safe for settlement.[12] Black soldiers were reported to be excellent, brave fighters, with some of the lowest desertion rates in the western armies. Black soldiers played important roles in fights with such legendary Indian leaders as Geronimo. One of the last great U.S. cavalry raids, the chasing of Pancho Villa into Mexico in 1916, was performed by black soldiers of the 10th Cavalry led by John J. "Black Jack" Pershing.[13] The exclusion of blacks from the U.S. cowboy story is a serious and unfortunate omission.

The factual errors in this myth are of more than scholarly interest. The symbols that serve the myth (the Marlboro man, Rambo, pickup trucks, Dirty Harry, guns, drinking, and smoking) and the macho attitudes held in imitation of these mythical figures (dislike of welfare recipients, homosexuals, unions, government, women professionals, and ethnic minorities) have profound policy impacts on us today. One wonders what some of the social and economic policies of such a state as Texas would look like if the cowboy myth had correctly incorporated the contributions of minorities, women, and governments and if it had placed in proper perspective the role of the individual cowboy.

The United States as God's Chosen Country

Religion has been and remains an important element of U.S. culture. The nation sees itself, and is seen by many in other lands, as the promised land, a nation blessed in resources and governmental form, a model society, and the modern world's Eden or at least a new version of Canaan. President Reagan has, as well as any modern-day American, expressed this view: "I have always believed that this anointed land was set apart in an uncommon way, that a divine plan placed this great continent here between the oceans to be found by people from every corner of the Earth who had a special love of faith and freedom."[14]

The speeches of U.S. presidents and of our lesser politicians are full of religious references and symbolism. Both the exaltation of God and calls for his guidance, patience, and understanding fill our political discussions. The link between politics and religion is so strong, and our attitude toward our political institutions is so reverent, that scholars have argued that politics in the United States is a true secular religion.[15] How do we reconcile this political religiosity with our fundamental value supporting the separation of church and state? As Bellah has argued,

The answer is that the separation of church and state has not denied the political realm of religious dimension. Although matters of personal religious belief, worship, and association are considered to be strictly private affairs, there are, at the same time, certain common elements of religious orientation that the great majority of Americans share. These have played a crucial role in the development of American institutions and still provide a religious dimension for the whole fabric of American life, including the political sphere. This public religious dimension is expressed in a set of beliefs, symbols and rituals that I am calling the American civil religion. The inauguration of a president is an important ceremonial event in this religion. It reaffirms, among other things, the religious legitimation of the highest political authority.[16]

This sanctified vision of the United States has seen us proclaim our manifest destiny in our westward expansion and our competition with other inhabitants of these lands. At the extremes, we have seen atheists denied rights to speak or to teach our children in public schools. We have even seen our school curriculum affected by conflicting scientific and religious versions of physical and historical events. We have heard Communists referred to as the Antichrist and we have seen the controversy over prayer in schools reach an importance few could have imagined in a secular country. We have witnessed the use of biblical interpretations of the roles of women and minorities to justify stereotyping, segregation, and opposition to birth control and abortion.

Religious symbols pervade U.S. political life. The Bible is a central prop in the swearing-in of our public officials. Prayers open and close most public events, including sessions of Congress. The pledge of allegiance not only unites us "under God," but is spoken with the reverence of a prayer.

Recognition of the religious myth is clearly important for our understanding of U.S. politics and public policies. Unlike the cowboy myth illustrated above, however, this one is not really subject to empirical validation or refutation. It deals in faith, questions of religious beliefs, and a spiritual linking of religious belief with governmental institutions and personages. Its hallmarks are self-righteousness, moral certainty, ethnocentrism, and cultural superiority. To discuss its merits and virtues is to engage in philosophical discourse, not empirical investigation. It is, therefore, a more difficult subject to deal with, if one opposes its interpreted prescriptions. As with all myths and symbols, however, no one group has a monopoly on the religious question, and different groups enbracing disparate views do compete for its mantle.

It may not be obvious at first glance why these particular myths and others like them have any direct relevance to U.S. politics. A closer examination, however, will show that such myths are important for determining how we feel about ourselves, how we view others, the relative contributions we think groups have made to our society, and what we think groups are entitled to expect from our political systems. The American cowboy myth, for example, supports a set of beliefs about individualism, self-help, the role of government, relationships with Native American populations, roles of men and women, and contributions of whites and blacks to the development of our nation that have strong public-policy implications. Similarly, the religious myths about our nation support a set of beliefs that link events to higher forces and causes, support some lifestyles over others, and favor certain moral and ethical systems, all of which have profound impacts on the direction of public policy in the United States. One can see, then, that if these seemingly apolitical myths play such an important part in public policy, more direct political myths must exert an even greater influence on the direction of our political policies and institutions. It is one set of such political myths and symbols—U.S. conservatism—that is the focus of this book.

CONSERVATISM AND PUBLIC POLICY IN THE UNITED STATES

Our political symbols and myths are derived from a general cultural consensus that legitimizes specific governmental policies and enables our political system to obtain the citizen support and compliance it needs to govern effectively. Our political disagreements are contained within a larger system of broad-based consensus. Without such agreement, societal conflicts would increase and important social, economic, and political resources would be spent on conflict management rather than on more important endeavors.

We Americans have not, however, arrived at our shared values and public policy orientations through uniformly personal and private logical processes. One hundred million U.S. voters did not independently, in their comfortable easy chairs, arrive at a set of political values and policy choices that happen to agree substantially with those of their near and distant fellow citizens. Our political socialization, the process by which we acquire our political values, is a community-influenced process. Families and friends, schools, churches, political leaders, political parties, the media, and governments themselves help shape our fundamental opinions about politics and government.[17]

In this process, children learn both directly through teaching and indirectly through imitation the basic myths, symbols, and values of our nation. One generation passes on its shared values and policy preferences to the next. Learning does not, however, stop when one reaches a certain age. And like all other learning, political learning is a lifelong process, wherein new information, new problems, and new opportunities may cause us individually and collectively to shift positions on important values and issues. It is part of human nature that we do not like to change our basic attitudes and values, but it is also human nature that under the right circumstances we can and do change them.[18] Broad-based policy changes, however, require persuasive communications, which may be more effective if appeals are linked to ongoing myths and symbols.

Because of the significant numbers of participants in the political learning process, it is not surprising that values change slowly, that fundamental shifts are rare, and that changes tend to affect large numbers of citizens at once. The forces at work leading one to rethink political values and policy preferences are also working on millions of other citizens. The result is that group changes are not unexpected or unprecedented. When these changes do occur, they will create pressure for change in the operation of government and politics.

Although their power has weakened in recent years, political parties continue to play an important role in manipulating U.S. primary and secondary myths and in translating them into public policy. Even with the growth in well-funded, narrowly focused ideological advocacy groups, parties continue to represent broad-based attitudinal positions within the population, and party fortunes reflect trends in ascendancy and descendancy of the various sets of secondary myths. Though their importance has diminished somewhat, political parties continue to be pragmatic organizers of politics, helping to bring centrality and direction out of a physically dispersed and ideologically and attitudinally diverse population. Because parties continue to play important roles in U.S. politics, and because they continue to reflect and represent broad, pragmatic trends within the electorate, scholars and practitioners pay close attention to the positions of our two major parties vis-à-vis the currently dominant political myths and symbols. They look especially for signs that might indicate any change in party balance, any change in public support for each party's package of public policies, and approaches that could signal major, long-term changes in U.S. public-policy agenda.

A party that is able to attract and successfully mobilize the majority of the electorate around its agenda can determine the fundamental directions U.S. public policy will take during that party's period of dominance. And the trend throughout our history has been for one or the other major party and its concomitant set of secondary myths, symbols, and policies to maintain its dominance for about 30 years. This is a significant period of time, during which a political party may have major short- and long-term influence on the public-policy directions of the country.

These periods of dominance, however, are definitely time-bound. Party identifications may weaken, new voters may enter the electorate, and realignments may occur in the relative attachment of citizens to the myths, symbols, and policies of the two major parties. Former minority parties may become majority parties, with concurrent changes in the direction of public policy in the United States. Or major parties may wane in influence as voters are captured by smaller, more issue-specific organizations. Scholars have identified four periods of party realignment in our history: the 1830s, the 1860s, the 1890s, and the 1930s.[19]

Our last major party realignment, with the ascendancy of the Democrats under Franklin D. Roosevelt, brought a more proactive set of public policies to prominence in the United States, one supporting greater government intervention in social and economic affairs. Like previous realignments, this one has had substantial staying power.

President Reagan and his administration have wished to facilitate a more ideologically conservative realignment in U.S. politics, and there are some signs that he may have moved us toward it: greater numbers and greater size of conservative organizations; more, and more prestigious, conservative publications; more, and more respected, conservative think tanks. There remains a question, however, as to how deeply these more elitist signs indicate the presence of a phenomenon that has filtered down to rank-and-file Americans. Early 1980s electoral and public opinion data indicate that this may be occurring.

The early 1980s saw marked increases in the electoral success of conservative Republican candidates. The broad-based victories of Reagan over Carter and over Mondale, the increases in Republican House and Senate strength, and the greater success of Republicans in state races were clear indicators of this movement. Public-opinion polls measuring political party identifications and ideological orientations showed a definite increase in conservatism and Republicanism. In 1977, 21 percent of the U.S. electorate identified themselves as Republicans, while 48 percent called themselves Democrats and 31 percent, Independents. Surveys conducted in the last three months of 1984 showed an increase among those calling themselves Republicans to 31 percent of the electorate, while those calling themselves Democrats decreased to 40 percent; Independents remained relatively stable at 29 percent.[20] Similar, although less pronounced, trends have

occurred in ideological orientations. When asked how they would define themselves—as liberals, moderates, or conservatives—voters sampled by the University of Michigan's Survey Research Center in their 1978 National Election
Study identified themselves as follows:[21]

Liberal	26 percent
Moderate	37 percent
Conservative	37 percent

By 1982, the last year for which complete Michigan data are available, these
percentages had changed to[22]

Liberal	23 percent
Moderate	35 percent
Conservative	42 percent

Although the changes are not overwhelming, the trend toward greater self-
identified conservatism is noticeable in these data. When we go beyond self-
described ideology to specific positions on important issues, we can see additional
evidence of the conservative shift in this period. A particularly salient conservative position is the belief that the government in Washington has become too
powerful. In 1970 only 44.2 percent of Americans agreed with this conservative
position; by 1980, the percentage had grown to about 75 percent.[23] Shifts like
these indicate the growing attraction of conservative views on government and
policy.

The early 1980s trends reported here are broad-based and national. Such figures
may mask even greater party and ideological shifting occurring among particular
pro-Democratic groups. Scholars who have looked specifically at southern whites
report a marked defection from their earlier Democratic loyalties. Douglas Gatlin,
writing in *Public Opinion Quarterly*, examined southern party identification
trends from 1952 to 1972 and reported substantial shifting occurring after 1964
and 1972, when white southerners dropped from 58 percent Democratic identification to 41 percent. During this same period, Republican identification rose
from 17 percent to 27 percent.[24] Long-term electoral comparisons show an even
more pronounced defection. "Whereas 85 percent of white Southerners voted
for FDR in 1936, just over a quarter of them backed Walter Mondale in 1984."[25]

Perhaps a more telling indicator of the conservative trend in this period was
the rhetoric of political debate. It is clear that in the late 1970s and early 1980s
the rhetoric of conservatism began to dominate discussions of public policy in
the United States. The term "liberal" became anathema. The conservative public
policy agenda of balanced budgets, reduced government services, greater defense
spending, decentralization of power, less government interference, and lower
taxes replaced the earlier liberal agenda of social services, equality, and an active
role for government in social and economic affairs. Again, one can see this

agenda movement clearly in the changing attitudes of voters toward the role of the federal government. Since 1964 the Survey Research Center at the University of Michigan has asked its National Election Study sample for its views on federal governmental power. In 1964 a minority of 46 percent of the electorate thought that the government in Washington was getting too powerful. By 1980, those thinking that the federal government was too powerful had increased to 76 percent.[26]

The ideologically based beliefs underlying what Reagan wished to see become the emerging conservative political consensus in the United States are simple and powerful and are tied to specific sets of social and economic governmental policies. Although there is obviously not monolithic agreement among all conservatives on the details of these beliefs, there is substantial agreement among many current conservative leaders and followers on a number of major assumptions and assertions about the U.S. society, the government, and the economic system. These positions, implicitly or explicitly expressed, can be found in the writings, speeches, political rhetoric, and public opinion surveys of U.S. conservatives. From a careful review of these sources, six basic conservative beliefs, or myths, can be identified:

1. Myth of the culture of poverty, which asserts that there are clearly superior and clearly inferior cultural values and that good values produce successful individuals and bad values produce unsuccessful individuals. Failure and success, therefore, can be predicted and explained on the basis of an individual's possession of proper or improper values.

2. Myth of the meritocracy, which asserts that those with better skills and the superior motivation emanating from their better values will succeed. Anyone with the appropriate skills and will can move up, regardless of the nature of the social, political, or economic environment.

3. Myth of decentralization, which argues that state and local governments are more efficient and are greater repositories of democratic values and institutions than is the national government.

4. Myth of the free market, which holds that the major positive strides in U.S. economic and social development come from the workings of the free market, not from regulations, planning, or any other type of government program or assistance. This myth also asserts that market competition is the most efficient and equitable mechanism for allocating goods and services in society.

5. Myth of federal government program and regulatory failure, which asserts that government social and economic programs have at best been ineffective and at worst have been harmful to those they were designed to help.

6. Myth of foreign economic success related to embracing conservative approaches and values, which argues that foreign economic successes, like those of Japan and Singapore, occur because these countries embrace basic conservative philosophies and programs and that we could do as well if we put these programs and approaches in place here.

Through the writings and speeches of conservative leaders and with reinforcement and guidance from a conservative president and administration, a set of myths, symbols, and policies that only a few years ago were supported by a minority of Americans may be on its way to becoming the dominant force in U.S. politics. This change may be appropriate. Citizens may be recognizing weakness in existing policy positions and deciding that they would be better off giving a Reagan-type conservative ideological agenda a try, but we should not stampede toward this new approach unthinkingly.

We citizens, and our consensus, are a battleground between competing political forces. The victor may determine the direction of U.S. society and politics for the next 50 years. The pre-Reagan position, supported for many years by a majority of U.S. citizens, argued for a relatively strong governmental role in the social and economic affairs of our nation. The result was a large number of government programs aimed at improving social and economic conditions for the more vulnerable strata of U.S. society. Social-welfare programs, labor-related legislation, social-security programs, medical-support programs, and a number of other government initiatives during this period sought to better the lives of large numbers of citizens through direct government intervention.

Conservatives charge that many of these programs were disruptive, costly, and often ineffective in achieving their goals.[27] Conservatives are quick to point out any deficiencies in these programs and to offer their own ideological approach as an alternative.[28] Although conservatives have consistently, and sometimes correctly, criticized liberal positions and policies, few have seriously examined the validity of the underlying assumptions and the ultimate policy consequences of the conservative position. The fact that previous policies may be wrong in certain areas does not automatically mean that the new conservative prescriptions are right. Things are not always simple either/ors in the complex world of politics and public policy. A possibility exists that many of the social, political, and economic underpinnings of conservative dogma may not stand the test of close empirical scrutiny.

And close empirical scrutiny is what is required if we are fairly and objectively to evaluate the merits of the various policy alternatives presented to us. President Reagan stressed the need for such analysis when he defended his administration's conservative positions against liberal attacks during the 1984 presidential campaign: ''The liberal old guard establishment—people who still make policies from abstract statistics, theories and models rather than looking at human behavior—have filled the airwaves with gloom, predicting our program couldn't meet our goals.''[29]

No one can argue that conservatives have been more prone than liberals to look at the facts. Each of us questions the beliefs and myths of others as a way of strengthening our positive feelings about our own choices. We like to think of ourselves as realists, pragmatists, down-to-earth kinds of folks who see things as they are. This is not a false view of ourselves, but it is not our only side. We may be realists, but we also have our emotional side. Our feelings are hurt when others do not see things as we do. Our myths, symbols, and policies are important to us, and we often justify them in emotional terms.

Few of us examine closely the validity of our own positions. To do so is more difficult than one might think, because so much emotional content surrounds these issues. It is not only what we see happening that is important, but it is also what we want to see happening. Because these issues and beliefs are so important, we must make an effort to be more objective and analytical in our approach to them. We must examine empirically the validity of ideologically supported programs and policies. The correctness of a policy, whether liberal or conservative, cannot simply be asserted on theoretical and emotional grounds or assumed because alternative policies have been shown to be flawed. Before the conservative myths, symbols, and policies ascend to dominance in U.S. politics, it is appropriate to take a hard look at the merits of this set of beliefs. Do these conservative beliefs represent a more correct view of people, institutions, and events, or are we being asked to accept a flawed explanation of our social, political and economic conditions?

The subsequent chapters of this book will examine the assumptions underlying the conservative myths. Citizens and politicians will then have more information to use in choosing among the competing myths, symbols, and public policies that will direct our lives into the next century.

NOTES

1. R. M. MacIver, *The Web of Government* (New York: Free Press, 1965), p. 4.

2. For a discussion of political cleavages see D. W. Rae and M. Taylor, *The Analysis of Political Cleavages* (New Haven, CT: Yale University Press, 1970).

3. See A. de Tocqueville, *Democracy in America* (New York: Washington Square Press, 1964); R. Hofstadter, *The American Political Tradition* (New York: Vintage Books, 1948); and W. Lippman, *The Public Philosophy* (New York: Mentor Books, 1955).

4. M. Edelman, *The Symbolic Uses of Politics* (Urbana: University of Illinois Press, 1964).

5. D. Nimmo and J. E. Combs, *Subliminal Politics: Myths and Mythmakers in America* (Englewood Cliffs, NJ: Prentice-Hall, 1980).

6. W. Lippmann, *Public Opinion* (New York: Free Press, 1965), p. 133.

7. For a discussion of the cowboy myth as portrayed in movies see J. H. Lenihan, *Showdown: Confronting Modern America in the Western Film* (Urbana: University of Illinois Press, 1980).

8. See, for example, A. Adams, *The Log of a Cowboy A Narrative of the Old Trail Days* (Lincoln: University of Nebraska Press, 1964); E. E. Dale, *Cow Country* (Norman: University of Oklahoma Press, 1965); J. B. Frantz and J. E. Choate, Jr., *The American Cowboy: The Myth and the Reality* (Norman: University of Oklahoma Press, 1955).

9. See D. T. Schoenberger, *The Gunfighters* (Caldwell, ID: Caxton Printers, 1971); and J. G. Rosa, *The Gunfighter: Man or Myth* (Norman: University of Oklahoma Press, 1977).

10. For a discussion of the positive role women played in the development of the West, see S. L. Myres, *Westering Women and the Frontier Experience, 1800–1915*

(Albuquerque: University of New Mexico Press, 1982); J. R. Jeffrey, *Frontier Women* (New York: Hill and Wang, 1979); and E. Richey, *Eminent Women of the West* (Berkeley, CA: Howell-North Books, 1975).

11. For information on the black cowboy experience see P. Durham and E. L. Jones, *The Negro Cowboys* (Lincoln: University of Nebraska Press, 1983); and K. W. Porter, "Negro Lab in the Western Cattle Industry, 1866–1900," *Labor History*. (Summer 1969): 346–74.

12. For a discussion of the black soldier in the west, see W. S. Savage, *Blacks in the West* (Westport, CT: Greenwood Press, 1976), pp. 48–64; and W. H. Leckie, *The Buffalo Soldiers: A Narrative of the Negro Cavalry in the West* (Norman: University of Oklahoma Press, 1967).

13. W. L. Katz, *The Black West* (Garden City, NY: Doubleday, 1971), p. 302.

14. Quote reported in *Newsweek*, December 27, 1982, p. 44.

15. See R. N. Bellah, "Civil Religion in America," *Daedalus* 96,(1) (Winter 1967); 1–21; and R. P. Hart, *The Political Pulpit* (West Lafayette, IN: Purdue University Press, 1977).

16. Bellah, "Civil Religion," pp. 3–4.

17. For a discussion of the political socialization process in the United States, see D. Easton and J. Dennis, *Children in the Political System* (New York: McGraw Hill, 1969); K. P. Langton, *Political Socialization* (New York: Oxford University Press, 1969); R. E. Dawson, K. Prewitt, and K. S. Dawson, *Political Socialization,* 2d ed. (Boston: Little, Brown, 1977); and R. S. Sigel, ed., *Learning about Politics* (New York: Random House, 1970).

18. For a discussion of the dynamics of attitude change see M. Fishbein and I. Ajzen, *Belief, Attitude, Intention and Behavior: An Introduction to Theory and Research* (Reading, MA: Addison-Wesley, 1975).

19. See W. D. Burnham, *Critical Elections and the Mainsprings of American Politics* (New York: Norton, 1970).

20. Gallup Report, January/February, 1985, p. 21.

21. University of Michigan, Survey Research Center, National Election Study, 1978.

22. University of Michigan, Survey Research Center, National Election Study, 1982.

23. Paul R. Abramson, *Political Attitudes in America: Formation and Change* (San Francisco: W. H. Freeman, 1983), p. 269.

24. D. S. Gatlin, "Party Identification, Status, and Race in the South: 1952–1972," *Public Opinion Quarterly* 38 (Spring 1975): 39–51.

25. E. C. Ladd, "As the Realignment Turns: A Drama in Many Acts," *Public Opinion* 7 (December/January 1985): 5.

26. University of Michigan, Survey Research Center, National Election Studies, 1964–80.

27. See A. J. Matusow, *The Unraveling of America*. New York: Harper & Row, 1984.

28. Some of the more popular works arguing this position are G. Gilder, *Wealth and Poverty* (New York: Basic Books, 1981); M. Friedman and R. Friedman, *Free to Choose* (New York: Harcourt Brace Jovanovich, 1980); C. Murray, *Losing Ground* (New York: Basic Books, 1984); and T. Sowell, *Ethnic America* (New York: Basic Books, 1981).

29. See Reagan remarks reported in *The Eagle,* College Station, Texas, August 18, 1984, p. 1.

2

A Question of Values

In every society there are some individuals and groups who are successful and some who are not. The more successful are those who achieve greater levels of wealth, greater occupational and social status, and higher levels of political influence. Explanations for differences in level of success range from political to economic, from cultural to religious. For U.S. conservatives, the differences in individual and group levels of achievement are explained primarily in cultural terms. The conservative mythology argues that there are clearly superior and clearly inferior cultural values and that good values produce successful individuals and groups and bad values produce unsuccessful individuals and groups. Conservatives, then, believe that people are essentially responsible for their own condition. Success or failure is inner-controlled, inner-determined, and linked to cultural values.

This is an attractive argument for a number of reasons. It presents us with a deterministic, controllable, moral, and predictable world. If we identify and adopt the correct values, we can succeed. It is within our power to control our destiny. For conservatives, then, the poor have caused their own condition and can rise above their disabilities only through the adoption of the correct values. The poor possess bad values that condemn them to poverty, from which they can escape only by changing themselves.

This argument, which is strongly supported by U.S. conservatives, is known as the culture-of-poverty thesis. It is a simple and powerful concept: The poor are responsible for their own condition; they have weak values, which differ from the superior values held by the successful; these weak values constitute a subculture of poverty, which is passed on from generation to generation; the only way to help the poor is to get them to change their values; external situational interventions will not do any good, because the problem originates within the individual and the group.

By bringing the cultural aspect to the success argument, conservatives have been doing more than emphasizing the internal focus of the problem of success and failure. They have been stressing their belief that the problem could be cast in larger group or class terms. For conservatives, "poverty was more than lack of income. [They were stressing] that various racial and ethnic groups responded differently to economic misfortune, that poor people did not necessarily want to act like the middle class, and that policymakers must be sensitive to the cultural gulf that separated lower-class groups from each other and from the rest of society."[1]

Placing the responsibility for poverty or failure directly on the shoulders of the individuals and groups afflicted is what William Ryan has termed "blaming the victim."[2] It is a posture that is almost as old as America itself. It was used by some people as early as the mid–1800s to explain why poor, free blacks lived in squalor in a particularly bad section of San Francisco.[3] The same argument was used 50 years later to explain why people live in poverty in the United States. Francis Walker, an economics professor who headed the U.S. Census Bureau, concluded in 1897 that "pauperism is largely voluntary. . . . Those who are paupers are so far more from character than from condition. They have the pauper trait; they bear the pauper brand."[4]

The serious development of the culture-of-poverty concept began with Professor Robert Park and the Chicago School of sociological analysis, which argued, as early as the mid–1920s, that "the patterns of the neighborhood, and the slum in particular, once they come into being, take on a life of their own and are to a great extent self-generated and self-perpetuating."[5] Although Park and his colleagues did not use the term "culture of poverty," they focused their explanations of urban poverty on the habits and customs of the poor, a fundamentally cultural or values approach.

The cultural aspects of the argument were made more explicit and the term culture of poverty was coined by Oscar Lewis in the 1960s.[6] From his participant-observation analyses of a few Mexican and Puerto Rican families, Lewis was convinced that his subjects suffered from and shared the values of a subculture of poverty. He argued that this condition affected not only the families he studied but applied to the poor elsewhere in these and other countries.[7] Lewis's linking of the behavior of a few families to the existence of widespread subcultures of poverty has been criticized by Charles Valentine in *Culture and Poverty*, in which he challenges the representativeness of Lewis's families and the generalizability of their behavior and values to others.[8] This criticism notwithstanding, the culture-of-poverty concept has become a focal point for liberals and conservatives alike in explaining behavioral differences between the poor and the nonpoor.

Other scholars and pundits took up the banner and added credibility and legitimacy to the culture-of-poverty argument, increasing its sophistication and appeal. It is from such advocates as Edward Banfield,[9] Irving Kristol,[10] George Gilder,[11] and Thomas Sowell[12] that the description of the poor as possessors of the culture of poverty becomes clear:

1. The poor are present-minded
2. The poor cannot defer gratification
3. The poor lack self-control
4. The poor lack the work ethic
5. The poor lack good work habits
6. The poor do not value education
7. The poor have pathological family structures and relationships
8. Poor parents pass these negative values to their children, making poverty inherited from generation to generation.

The conclusion is that the poor fail because of characteristics within themselves, not because of the actions of others or external, situational factors. The poor share a set of values, different from those of the nonpoor, that are negative and are responsible for their poverty. The causal arrow points in one direction, from bad values to poverty. Therefore, any program for change must come from within the poor, not from such external actions as government social-welfare programs.

The culture-of-poverty thesis and the portrait of the poor it paints are attractive and compelling both because of their simplicity and because they are so ideologically pleasing to powerful groups of U.S. citizens. The argument, however, is demonstrably wrong. The following pages will show that the issues of poverty and success are more complicated than the conservatives would have us believe.

Let us begin our analysis by looking carefully at what the conservative proponents are saying and what evidence they are presenting to make their case.[13] Two general categories of scholarly proponents can be identified, who espouse most or all of the elements of the conservative position that cultural values are the basis of successful or unsuccessful competition in society. In the first category, the academically oriented conservative scholars, are individuals who write primarily for a scholarly audience.[14] A leading advocate of the conservative position in this category is Professor Edward Banfield of Harvard University.

The second category is made up of scholars or professional writers who, while they may be interested in scholarly discourse, have a powerful interest in influencing public attitudes and government decision makers. Although such individuals may have university connections, they are generally affiliated with ideologically based foundations and publications, and they tend to become public figures and spokesmen for conservative positions.[15] Their principal audience is usually not the community of scholars but public officials, opinion leaders, and a more mass audience. A leader of this group is Thomas Sowell, an economist affiliated with the conservative Hoover Institution in Palo Alto, California.

The writings and speeches of members of both of these categories contain a full complement of the conservative homilies, positions, and assertions about the nature of poverty and the proper responsibility for it. To provide the fullest examination of the validity of the conservative position on this issue, it is worthwhile to evaluate the arguments and data of two principal advocates, Banfield and Sowell.

EDWARD BANFIELD: THE UNHEAVENLY THEORY

In the late 1960s Edward Banfield, professor of government at Harvard University, published *The Unheavenly City*, which asserts the existence of class subcultures, including a lower-class culture of poverty.[16] His argument is, on the surface, relatively simple. People can be divided into cultural classes based on values, particularly values toward the future. For Banfield, all success- and failure-related behavior derives from an individual's orientation to the future. Two factors are of importance: the individual's ability to imagine a future, and the individual's ability to discipline himself or herself to deny present benefits for future rewards.[17]

In Banfield's scheme, all success-related values and behaviors stem from the presence or absence (including degrees of presence or absence) of these two factors. Using these factors as guides, he divides the U.S. citizenry into four classes: the upper class, which exhibits the most future-oriented behavior; the middle class, which exhibits the next highest future-oriented behavior; the working class, which exhibits less future-oriented behavior than the others, but which still possesses some future-oriented capability; and the lower class, which is essentially present oriented.

For Banfield, it is one's orientation toward the future and the values associated with such an orientation that lead to the behaviors that bring success or failure in one's life. The causal arrow runs one way in Banfield's scheme, from values to poverty or nonpoverty status. Placed in class terms, success is the natural outgrowth of the better values held by the upper classes; poverty is the natural outgrowth of the inferior values held by the lower classes. Poverty, therefore, is the effect—not the cause—of the lower-class culture.[18]

Like the culture-of-poverty advocates before and since, Banfield goes on to argue that because the problems of poverty are the result of inadequacies among the poor people themselves, there is little that can or should be done externally to correct the situation:

Lower-class poverty . . . is "inwardly" caused [by psychological inability to provide for the future, and all that this inability implies]. Improvements in external circumstances can affect this poverty only superficially. . . . In principle, it is possible to eliminate the poverty (material lack) of such a family, but only at great expense, since the capacity of the radically improvident to waste money is almost unlimited. Raising such a family's income would not necessarily improve its way of life, moreover, and could conceivably even make things worse. . . .

So long as the city contains a sizable lower class, nothing basic can be done about its most serious problems. Good jobs may be offered to all, but some will remain chronically unemployed. Slums may be demolished, but if the housing that replaces them is occupied by the lower class it will shortly be turned into new slums. Welfare payments may be doubled or tripled and a negative income tax instituted, but some persons will continue to live in squalor and misery. New schools may be built, new curricula devised, and the teacher–pupil ratio cut in half, but if the children who attend these schools come from lower-class homes, they will be turned into blackboard jungles, and those who graduate or drop out from them will in most cases, be functionally illiterate. . . . If however, the lower class were to disappear—if, say, its members were overnight to acquire the attitudes, motivations and habits of the working class—the most serious and intractable problems of the city would all disappear with it.[19]

Again, it is easy to see the attractiveness to conservatives of Banfield's position. The reason people act badly or don't succeed is that they have bad values. Any improvements must come from within. Therefore, there is little need for us to do anything to help, such as spend money on programs, because they will surely fail.

The problem is that this argument is fundamentally circular. Nowhere in Banfield's presentation are values, or orientations, measured at some early point and then the successes and failures of individuals possessing different values predicted and subsequently evaluated. We are told only that differential rates of success and failure are present in society. Only because Banfield asserts it are we to know that these differences are caused by the possession of different values. Banfield's argument reduces to this: Why do certain people succeed? Because they have the right values. How do we know they have the right values? Because they have succeeded. Why do other people fail? Because they have the wrong values. How do we know they have the wrong values? Because they have failed.

This is arguing backward. A true theory of behavior must predict forward, not backward. The method of science requires that we know *a priori* which people, because of their values, will succeed or fail. It is not enough to start with successes and failures and *a posteriori* assert that the differences noted are caused by different values.

Yet this is exactly what Banfield does. He is essentially asking us to accept on faith his assertion that the differences we observe among people, on questions relating to education, family life, work, criminal behavior, and political behavior, are the result of class-based value differences. His interpretations of the differences he notes among people on such variables as education and political participation never empirically address the presence or absence of particular values among the groups or classes that are exhibiting particular behaviors.

One may agree with Banfield that people do differ on a number of educational, political, and other behaviors and may also agree that some of these behavioral differences may be associated with class status, but here is where the agreement ends. There are other compelling explanations for these differences that are not based on values. All Banfield has offered, to provide grounds for a class-based values explanation of observed behavioral differences, is his own assertion that it is so.

His way out of the circular box he has constructed is to convince us that his original classification scheme is so strong, so based on irrefutable and convincing evidence, that it lends validity to all his later interpretations, which, while not directly measuring values, do depend on the values scheme and premise established in the original classifications. To provide any possible legitimacy for his later assertions, Banfield must convince the reader of the correctness of his basic classification scheme. To evaluate his position, then, we must go back to Banfield's original classifications. We must see if they are built on a sound foundation of logic and empirical work and if they provide convincing evidence of class-based values that clearly differentiate segments of society and stand as the principal antecedents of the educational, political, familial, and other behaviors he associates with success and failure.

In attempting to make his point and build a predictive, class-based model of society, Banfield presents a surprisingly small amount of empirical evidence. He offers no original data of his own. All of his arguments and justifications are based on his interpretation of the works of other scholars in other contexts. Therefore, to evaluate Banfield's position, we must assess the appropriateness, content, and interpretations of the works he cites to support his theory. When we turn to these other studies, we find that they are limited. The relatively few studies cited raise serious questions about their appropriateness for this discussion and for the interpretations and conclusions Banfield draws.

Banfield's argument is a cultural-values one. People of four distinct classes— upper, middle, working, and lower—share values that cause their success or failure. The only broadly based, empirical work Banfield cites that directly addresses the motion of class-based values is a 1959 study by Melvin Kohn published in the *American Journal of Sociology*.[20] Although Banfield cites this work to further his claim for the existence of a distinct upper class, Kohn includes no upper class in his sample. His study also has no lower class. It compares some values orientations of the middle and working classes. In examining the sample and the findings of Kohn's study of middle- and working-class individuals, we see that they do not merit the position Banfield has given them as a keystone of his class-based theory.

Kohn's study examines about 400 families in the Washington, DC area. Kohn interviewed the mother in each family and the father and a child in one out of four families. Because of the small sample size for fathers, we will follow Kohn's lead and focus on the sample of mothers, although the findings for fathers are not very different. Kohn asked his sample of mothers to select from a list of 17 characteristics he provided them those they would most like to see in their

Table 2.1

Proportion of Mothers Who Selected Each Characteristic as One of Three "Most Desirable" in a 10- or 11-Year-Old Child

	Combined Boys and Girls	
Characteristics	Middle Class Mothers	Working Class Mothers
1. That he is honest	.44	.53
2. That he is happy	.46*	.36
3. That he is considerate of others	.39*	.27
4. That he obeys his parents well	.20*	.33
5. That he is dependable	.24	.21
6. That he has good manners	.19	.24
7. That he has self control	.22*	.13
8. That he is popular with other children	.15	.18
9. That he is a good student	.15	.17
10. That he is neat and clean	.11*	.20
11. That he is curious about things	.18*	.06
12. That he is ambitious	.07	.13
13. That he is able to defend himself	.10	.06
14. That he is affectionate	.05	.04
15. That he is liked by adults	.05	.04
16. That he is able to play by himself	.01	.02
17. That he acts in a serious way	.00	.01

*Social class differences statistically significant, 0.05 level or better, using chi-squared test.

Source: Melvin L. Kohn, "Social Class and Parental Values," <u>American Journal of Sociology</u>, <u>64</u>, (4), p. 339.

children. The findings of this question from Kohn's article are presented in Table 2.1.

In looking at these data, the reader will come to the same conclusion that Kohn did, namely, the middle- and working-class parents share a broad set of values. Mothers in both groups tend to prize honesty, happiness, consideration, obedience, and dependability and to downplay most other characteristics in similar proportions. There are some small differences, but these are really of degree, not of kind. It is difficult to see why or how Banfield chose this study as one on which to base his class argument.

The reader might correctly say that this is a small sample in only one area of the country. Although Banfield inappropriately cites this study as supporting his position, it is possible that more representative data would provide more support

Table 2.2
Proportion of Respondents Who Select Each Characteristic as the "Most Desirable" or One of Three "Most Desirable" (the two categories are summed to get the total proportion selecting each characteristic)

Characteristic	Welfare	Non-Welfare
Studiousness	.050	.052
Manners	.259	.236
Success	.140	.134
Honesty	.676	.681
Cleanliness	.088	.071
Judgment	.372	.377
Self-control	.165	.179
Interest/curiosity	.167	.156
Amicability	.130	.131
Obedience	.326	.301
Responsibility	.303	.343
Considerate	.265	.295
N	2880	5167

Source: Table computed from data provided by General Social Surveys, 1972-1984, National Opinion Research Center.

for his point. Let us look at the kind of data Banfield might have presented to evaluate his assertion of the existence of unique, class-based values.

For each year during the past several decades, the National Opinion Research Center (NORC), in conjunction with the Roper Public Opinion Research Center, has conducted and made available to scholars national studies on social issues and values based on questionnaires administered to national samples of the U.S. population.[21] The findings of several of these studies are periodically aggregated, so that scholars can use large data sets collected over time to evaluate dimensions of social behavior and values among the citizenry. These studies ask questions about desirable characteristics similar to those Kohn asked his much smaller sample of Washington, DC mothers. These General Social Surveys, as they are called, also ask whether the respondent has ever been on welfare, an important and particularly relevant indicator to help us divide the population into the class categories so important to Banfield.

Table 2.2 presents the findings of the General Social Surveys, cumulated for the period 1972–84, on the desirability of 12 characteristics arrayed by welfare or nonwelfare status of the respondent.

Examining the findings of Table 2.2 makes it clear that no fundamental value differences exist between welfare and nonwelfare respondents. The proportions supporting the various characteristics are almost identical for both categories.

These broader, more representative national studies, like Kohn's, not only provide no support for Banfield's position but they also directly contradict it.

It is true that neither the general social survey data nor Kohn's data directly tap the future-orientation idea that is advanced as so important by Banfield. In his own narrative, Banfield cites only one empirical study to support this future-oriented/present-oriented dichotomy. Banfield notes: "The working-class individual does not 'invest' as heavily in the future, nor in so distant a future, as does the middle-class one."[22] Following this statement, Banfield cites, as justification, a passage from an article by Basil Bernstein in a 1958 issue of the *British Journal of Sociology*.[23]

Turning to this work by Bernstein, we might expect to see a comparison on future-oriented issues of middle-class and working-class individuals. We are left disappointed. First, the work by Bernstein is not comparative at all. The data he presents are of working-class youth only. Second, the work does not directly test values oriented toward the future; rather, the data relate working-class-youth I.Q. scores to vocabulary competencies. The passage Banfield cites to bolster his present-oriented/future-oriented argument is an untested assertion by Bernstein that is unrelated to the empirical analysis he performed in his study. Thus, the evidence Banfield offers is nothing more than the citation of an unsubstantiated assertion by another author.

Other scholars have more directly and completely addressed the question of whether class-based, present and future values orientations exist. One of these is a study by social psychologist Milton Rokeach and anthropologist Seymour Parker.[24] Although Rokeach and Parker, unlike Kohn and this author, do find some value areas in which poor and nonpoor differ, they make it clear that these differences do not include future and present orientations:

Our data, however, do not provide support for the widely held belief that the culture of the poor is characterized by present oriented, hedonistic values. We find no differences between the poor and the rich on "an exciting life" or on "pleasure." Both of these values are ranked well toward the bottom of the terminal value scale by poor and rich alike. Moreover, the idea that the poor value immediate gratification more than the rich does not receive support from the NORC data.[25]

What, then, is one to conclude from a close inspection of the foundations of Banfield's classification scheme? It is clear from the studies cited by Banfield himself, from the additional data provided by Rokeach and Parker, and from the General Social Surveys that there is simply no empirically based justification for the class-based classification scheme advanced by Banfield.

THOMAS SOWELL: WEST INDIAN MYTHS AND IMMIGRANT REALITIES

Thomas Sowell is a black economist who works at the prestigious conservative think tank, the Hoover Institution, in Palo Alto, California. He has argued forcefully and publicly for the conservative public policy agenda so popular in the United States today. His positions include opposition to almost all direct-action government programs aimed at improving the lot of the poor, especially poor blacks, in U.S. society.

Like other conservative spokespersons, Sowell embraces the culture-of-poverty thesis that poverty is essentially self-generated, the result of inferior cultural values. He comes to this conclusion from a perspective similar to that of Banfield. Both Banfield and Sowell begin with the observation of different rates of success for various groups, and both assert that these observed differences can be explained by the different cultural values possessed by the members of these groups.

Like Banfield, Sowell never directly measures value differences among the groups he compares. Unlike Banfield, however, Sowell does attempt to present indirect evidence of his own, principally aggregate census data, to show that groups that have achieved different levels of success may have done so because of differentially held values. My summary of the core of Sowell's argument, as presented in his several publications, follows.[26]

Different ethnic and racial groups have existed in the United States for generations. Over the years, most of these groups have been able to make substantial improvements in their economic situations, that is, become more successful. One particular group—American blacks—has not participated fully in this fundamental U.S. success story. Most of the successful groups have faced hostile situations not dissimilar to those faced by American blacks, yet they have prevailed, while Americn blacks have not. The only way to account for these differential success stories, given similar obstacles, is to conclude that the more successful groups possessed attitudes and values superior to those possessed by American blacks. The only way for American blacks to better their situations, therefore, is through self-improvement programs and the acquisition of better values.

Sowell expresses this view in *Race and Economics:*

Some traits commonly thought of as causes of economic failure and social pathology are low-income origins, overcrowded and substandard housing, prejudice and discrimination, inadequate educational opportunities, and a general failure of public services. . . . All those things impeded the progress of all American minorities; but it is by no means clear that the more successful minorities had any less of such handicaps than the less successful minorities. . . .

It would be very difficult to discover any relationship between the different rates of economic advance by different minorities and the various "causes" of poverty. However, it is not so difficult to relate the rate of advance of certain cultural traits. Among the characteristics associated with success is a future orientation—a belief in a pattern of behavior that sacifices present comforts and enjoyments while preparing for future success. This may manifest itself in building up a business, acquiring a skilled trade, or in long years of educational preparation for a professional or intellectual career. Those groups who did this . . . all came from social backgrounds in which this kind of behavior was common before they set foot on American soil. . . .

A high value on immediate "fun" "excitement," and emotionalism has characterized the less successful minorities. . . .

There are, apparently, traits that do and traits that do not produce economic advance, and there are historical conditions that do and do not produce these traits in various groups.[27]

Can one really say that nonblack ethnic groups faced the same handicaps as American blacks? Sowell wants to persuade us that values, not situational limits, are the cause of success and failure. He must, therefore, prove to us that the negative environment that existed for American blacks was shared by other, more successful ethnic groups. Sowell attempts to do this by introducing what I call the "West Indian factor."

Sowell realizes that it would be difficult to persuade us that white Irish or Italian ethnics, or Asian Japanese and Chinese ethnics, faced conditions of hostility and discrimination similar to those of American blacks, although this is clearly his position. Their success is noteworthy, but alone it is not enough to condemn the values of American blacks. Recognizing this vulnerability in his argument, Sowell presents for comparison a group that, he argues, is essentially the same in characteristics as American blacks, a group so similar that they can be said to have faced similar negative economic and social conditions, yet to have succeeded where American blacks have failed.

Sowell believes that the West Indian black immigrants to the United States are such a group. According to him, this group has faced economic hardship and social rejection similar to that faced by American blacks, yet they have succeeded. Sowell then asserts his preferred conclusion, namely, that negative environments do not limit individual or group success. Rather, the limits to success come from the bad values within.

To illustrate his point that other ethnic groups, especially West Indian blacks, have succeeded, while American blacks have failed, Sowell presents aggregate statistics comparing the economic accomplishments of various American ethnic groups as measured by median family income. The aggregate data that Sowell uses as the basis for his assertions is presented in Table 2.3.

They key comparison in this table, as far as Sowell's basic argument is concerned, is between West Indians and American blacks, who earn 94 percent and 62 percent, respectively, of the U.S. average. Here, according to Sowell, is the irrefutable empirical evidence that West Indian blacks, who faced conditions similar to those faced by American blacks, have significantly outstripped black Americans in accomplishments. And how does Sowell explain these superior accomplishments? He does so by pointing out the better values West Indian blacks brought to the United States from their West Indian roots.

Sowell finds the source of these superior roots in the slave culture of West Indian blacks:

In short, the most bitterly criticized features of slavery—callous overwork, sexual exploitation, Negro fragmentation, and self-denigration of blackness—were worse in the

Table 2.3
Family Income Index, 1970 (U.S. average = 100)

Jewish	172
Japanese	132
Polish	115
Chinese	112
Italian	112
German	107
Anglo-Saxon	107
Irish	103
TOTAL U.S.	100
Filipino	99
West Indian	94
Mexican	76
Puerto Rican	63
Black	62
Indian	60

Source: U.S. Bureau of the Census; National Jewish
          Population Survey. (Reprinted from Thomas
          Sowell, Ethnic America, p. 5.)

West Indies than in the United States. However, several other features of West Indian
slavery that have received less attention may help explain the greater success of West
Indians in the United States. Unlike slaves in the United States who were issued food
rations and were often fed from the common kitchen, West Indian slaves were assigned
land and time to raise their own food. They sold surplus food in the market to buy
amenities for themselves. In short, West Indian Negroes had centuries of experience in
taking care of themselves in a significant part of their lives, even under slavery, as well
as experience with buying and selling. . . . They had the kind of incentives and experience
common in a market economy but denied American slaves for two centuries.[28]

It is certainly possible for us to take issue with many of Sowell's assertions
about the factors underlying the accomplishments of the ethnic groups he examines. One author, Stephen Steinberg, points out several important skill and
environmental-context issues that cast serious doubts on the validity of Sowell's
assertions about the superior cultural values of nonblack ethnic groups as the
source of their accomplishments.[29] Because, however, the heart of Sowell's
culture-of-poverty argument rests on his comparisons of the accomplishments
of West Indian and American blacks, that is where this present evaluation will
be focused.

There are a number of flaws and omissions in Sowell's comparisons of West
Indian and American blacks that render his conclusions suspect. We will first
look at the groups Sowell is comparing. One group consists of black West Indian

immigrants and their offspring, approximately 200,000 individuals, most of whom live in and around New York City. The other group is made up of 20 million American blacks, spread throughout the United States with the largest concentrations in the South and in urban areas of the Midwest and East. So what Sowell is presenting is a comparison of a relatively small, homogeneous, geographically concentrated, self-selected group of West Indian blacks and a much larger, heterogeneous, geographically dispersed, non-self-selected group of American blacks.

The obvious question is whether this is an appropriate comparison to use in attempting to draw conclusions about group values and cultural underpinnings affecting success and failure, when one's only indicator is mean family income. The answer is a resounding no. And the reason is neither complicated nor obscure. We know that individuals and groups differ in their economic accomplishments. There are many plausible explanations for this: Some have more relevant education and skills, some face more restrictive environments, some have superior cultural values, and some evidence a combination of these factors. Culture is considered in most social scientists' analyses, and especially in those like Sowell's where cultural indicators are not directly measured, as a residual explanatory category. If he, or we, can explain observable differences in level of accomplishment with the more simple, straightforward, and directly measured explanation of situational context, we have no need to infer cultural differences as a causal factor. To be sure that culture and not a set of external situationally based factors is responsible for observable differences between comparison groups, we must present comparisons that control for these other variables. Only then can we be sure that observed differences may be cultural, not situational, in origin.

The problem is that Sowell does not control for these contextual variations. On the contrary, they are the heart of his comparison. The uncontrolled comparison he provides of West Indian and American blacks cannot answer the cultural question Sowell wants it to. It is like comparing the income levels of Yale graduates with the income levels of state university graduates in the United States, finding differences, and arguing that the Yalies have greater incomes because they have superior cultural values. Few conclusions would be more absurd or inappropriate, but this is what Sowell is asking us to believe in his parallel and equally inappropriate comparison of West Indian and American blacks.

Neither our Yale comparison nor Sowell's racial comparison adequately controls for the situational factors that must be considered if a cultural explanation is to be either needed or appropriate. The only proper scientific approach is to look at American and West Indian blacks in similar contexts. If differences persist, then culture can be considered as an explanation.

When the proper comparisons are made, the differences Sowell sees begin to disappear. In situations similar (in locaction or educational level) to those of the geographically concentrated West Indian blacks, American blacks do much better

Table 2.4
Mean Family Income Comparisons of Post-High School Educated American
Blacks and West Indians Living in the New York/New Jersey SMSA

	American Blacks	West Indians
Mean Family Income	$21,328.70	$19,107.90

Source: U.S. Bureau of the Census, *Census Population and Housing 1980: Public-Use Microdata Sample* (Washington, DC: Bureau of the Census, 1983).

vis-à-vis West Indians on such dimensions as family income. Sowell himself is not unaware of the problems inherent in the type of comparison he is making:

Something as apparently innocuous as location has a great impact on income. Regional differences in incomes are very substantial, especially as between the South and other regions. The average difference in income between California and Arkansas is greater than that between blacks and whites. Between Alaska and Mississippi, the income difference is greater still. The apparent paradox that Puerto Ricans earn a shade more than blacks nationally, while at any given location blacks tend to earn more than Puerto Ricans, is easily explained by the fact that half the black population of the United States is located in the low-income South.[30]

Even Sowell has demonstrated that the difference in income he observes between West Indians and American blacks may, in fact, be less when proper controls are applied. In his book chapter "Three Black Histories" (1978) he presents a table comparing the personal incomes of northern blacks, southern blacks, and West Indians with four years of college.[31] The similarity of incomes of comparably educated northern blacks and West Indians is startling: $7,330 and $7,662, respectively, with southern college-educated blacks trailing far behind at $5,887. The regional effect on black income accomplishments is unmistakable in this finding. And even though Sowell notes this "shrinking" gap for northern American blacks, rather than view this finding as an indication of the importance of taking into account regional and educational factors when making West Indian and American black comparisons, he simply persists in his basic argument that observed income differences denote West Indian cultural superiority.

In fact, when an even more appropriate comparison is made between regionally similar post-high-school-educated (one year of college or more) West Indian and American blacks, the findings indicate that American blacks actually do *better* than their West Indian counterparts. Table 2.4 presents 1980 census data comparing the mean family incomes (mean family income has consistently been the principal measure used by Sowell to make his intergroup comparisons) of post-high-school-educated American blacks and West Indians living in the New York/

New Jersey SMSA. Sowell has correctly told us that the majority of West Indians live in and around New York City. To properly compare the accomplishments of comparably situated American blacks and West Indians, the most appropriate comparison is not with *all* northern blacks, as Sowell did, but with American blacks having experiences and environments similar to those faced by their West Indian competitors. These American blacks would also live in and around New York City. As the income figures in Table 2.4 indicate, post-high-school-educated American blacks in the New York/New Jersey SMSA seem to have substantially *higher* family incomes than do similarly educated West Indians in the same SMSA.

After replicating Sowell's analysis, comparing more appropriate geographical groups, we find the differences he noted among college-educated blacks and West Indians disappear. But what about other levels of education? Do blacks or West Indians in the New York/New Jersey metropolitan area, with levels of education less than college, have differential mean-family-income accomplishments? This is a difficult question to answer, and the answer will raise important doubts about any mean-family-income comparisons made by Sowell or anyone else between categories of American and West Indian blacks.

The problem is a statistical one and relates to problems generated by small sample sizes. People tend to think that when one deals with comparisons of census data, one is dealing with huge populations where problems of sampling are not relevant. This is not always the case, however. Data about ethnicity and family income, such as those selected by Sowell for his comparisons, are from census public-use samples. Not every black and every West Indian in the United States is included in these samples. In fact, only one out of every thousand census respondents is included in these public-use samples made available by the Census Bureau for this kind of analysis.

So of the 200,000 or so West Indians in the United States, only one in 1,000 or about 200, should be represented in this particular census-data file. In fact, because of sampling, age differentiations, or other factors in determining census sample distributions, the 1980 Census Public-Use Microdata Sample, from which comparisons like Sowell's and mine must be drawn, contains only 161 West Indians. When one further focuses the analysis on the New York/New Jersey area, the available sample of West Indians drops to only 88.

Now, making mean comparisons between sample groups when one or both of them have small n's is fraught with problems. The key question is, with such small samples, how can one be certain that the mean figure found in the sample truly represents the actual mean figure for the overall population group? When one has a small sample, such as one with only 88 West Indians, one cannot be sure that the mean for any value, such as family income, found in the sample is the true value of the larger population. One can be confident only that the true population value falls within a range of values including the mean reported in the sample. Statisticians have developed a formula to report this range, or confidence interval, for interpreting mean values found in samples, and this range increases as sample size decreases and as the variance in values of sample respondents' answers increases:[32]

$$\overline{x} = \pm 1.9 \times \frac{S\,D}{\sqrt{n-1}}$$

where true population mean $= \pm 1.9$ times standard deviation divided by square root of sample size minus 1.

What this formula tells us is that in small samples, particularly ones where the variation in the answers of the sample respondents is large, the confidence interval of the true population value is quite large; that is, the mean value reported for the sample is not very useful in making comparisons in these cases.

Going back to our area educational comparisons illustrates the problem. The census sample for New York/New Jersey includes only 17 West Indians with an elementary education, 43 with a high-school education, and 28 with a college education. The sample numbers for American blacks in the same area were 57 elementary, 238 high school, and 81 college. In fact, samples for both groups are relatively small, standard deviations for the mean family income for the sub groups are relatively large, and the resulting confidence intervals for the true population means for family income across education categories for both groups are large—ranging from plus or minus $1,329 to $3,063 for American blacks to plus or minus $3,934 to $5,029 for West Indians.

This means that if one finds a sample family-income mean for one group of New York/New Jersey West Indians of $15,000, the true area West Indian population family-income mean for that group actually lies between $10,000 and $20,000. The same problem, on only a slightly lesser scale, exists for our New York/New Jersey American blacks. The reader can immediately see the problem that exists in comparing sample means in cases like this and assuming that they indicate the true population mean, when in fact the true population mean lies within a huge range, in this example $10,000.

How is the reader, then, to interpret a finding of sample family-income means of say $15,000 for a West Indian group and $13,000 for an American black group? As we have demonstrated, one cannot, as Sowell does, assume from this simple comparison that the West Indian population group has a higher income achievement level than the American black population. The true mean for the West Indian population group lies within a range of $10,000 to $20,000, while that of the American black group lies between $10,000 and $16,000. We cannot know from the data presented whether the true mean family income for either group is higher, lower, or the same as that for the other group. Anyone who asserts otherwise is ignoring the important statistical realities discussed above. It becomes clear, then, that when more thoughtful and more statistically correct comparisons are made, the income differences that Sowell and the conservatives use to argue for a culturally inferior American black population are simply inappropriate and inaccurate.

So far, we have dealt only with the legitimacy of the comparison Sowell offers, that between West Indian and American blacks. And we have seen that his cultural assertions deflate under proper considerations. There is another comparison, however, one not discussed by Sowell, that further flattens his cultural argument. This is a simple comparison of the relative accomplishments of various West Indian populations. After all, few West Indians have emigrated to the United States. Much larger groups of West Indians either emigrated to Britain or remained in the West Indies. All three West Indian groups—those who came to the United States, those who went to Britain, and those who stayed home— have the same culture, according to Sowell, an achievement culture superior to that of American blacks.

Yet, when we look at the achievements of these three groups we find them extremely varied. West Indians in the United States do better than West Indians in Britain who, in turn, do better than West Indians who remain at home. And, contrary to what Sowell asserts about American West Indians, West Indians in Britain do substantially worse than other British ethnic groups.[33] Culture cannot explain the intragroup West Indian differences, because the culture is the same for all three West Indian groups. The differences are clearly situational. What is important is who emigrated, who stayed, and what situational context they faced.

Summarizing, then, we find no merit in Sowell's cultural argument. More proper comparisons of West Indian and American blacks show that there are no residual differences that need explaining by any cultural concept. Internal West Indian comparisons show that differences persist, even when culture is held constant. Nothing Sowell has presented indicates that either significant cultural differences exist between West Indians and American blacks or that cultural arguments explain any differences in the relative success or failure of West Indians and American blacks.

What is both fascinating and disturbing about Sowell's work is that he is not unaware of these flaws and omissions. Most of the points I have raised are evident even in his own analyses. The problem is that they are simply dismissed and are never incorporated in or related to his basic proposition. Their importance and significance for his assertions are ignored. For example, he extols at length the superiority of West Indian blacks and the cultural nature of this superiority. He provides detailed descriptions of the slave environment purportedly producing these differences. Then, in a sentence or two, he adds something that totally contradicts his entire argument.

He presents these points casually, and their implications are never seriously discussed. Consider, for example, the following passages from the end of Chapter 4 of *The Economics and Politics of Race*. Throughout this chapter Sowell has extolled and reported the greater achievements of West Indian blacks in the

United States and has assigned these accomplishments almost exclusively to cultural superiority. Then he adds:

> West Indian immigrants in London were not nearly so successful, perhaps because they have arrived later, or because they did not have a large native black population to provide customers for their businesses, clienteles for their professions, or voting support for their political leaders. Nor are West Indians prosperous in their homelands. The per capita output (real income) of Trinidad is less than that of Puerto Rico and only 28 percent of that of the United States. The per capita output of Jamaica is only about half that of Trinidad.[34]

These statements strike at the heart of his culture-based argument, yet they are presented as extraneous bits of trivia. Other scholars of minority experiences in Great Britain, however, point out the serious social, political, and economic problems minority groups encountered and how these environmental difficulties affected their levels of success.[35]

THE POVERTY OF CULTURE

The inescapable conclusion drawn from our evaluation of the positions articulated by the representatives of the culture-of-poverty thesis is that these positions are largely without merit. The values they argue determine success and poverty cannot be shown to exist, much less to have solely accounted for anyone's success or failure. We have seen that the data and arguments presented by conservative scholars and professional advocates of the culture-of-poverty thesis cannot stand scrutiny. The evidence is overwhelming that other factors—not distinct, class-based values—must be the principal causes of success and failure in American society.

The weaknesses that have been pointed out in the arguments of Banfield and Sowell have not prevented these arguments from becoming accepted and extolled by other conservative writers, commentators, and politicians. Error feeds on error, as conservatives cite each other's misinformation and misinterpretations in their attempts to frame policies to blame the poor for the existence of poverty and hardship. The error is compounded through others who embrace and use as their justification general or specific elements of the culture-of-poverty myth.

Consider, for example, the position taken by Irving Kristol in an article prepared for the twenty-fifth anniversary edition of *The Public Interest*. On the basis of the erroneous assertions of Sowell regarding the superiority of West Indian culture and accomplishments, Kristol tells us that we need to adopt West Indian education methods: "But experience has taught us that working-class and slum children *need* the more traditional, 'structured' schools. That this is so is suggested by the fact that black immigrants from the slums of the West Indies—where the schools are 'old fashioned' in a British way—end up doing much better, economically and socially, than their American-born counterparts."[36]

Without any measured analyses or data, but simply because of Sowell's initial errors, Kristol would have us adopt a West Indian school system that has consistently produced less successful individuals than that of any major urban school system in the United States. Here is error merging with ideological bias to suggest a wholly inappropriate and unjustified public policy.

This is merely one example of how specific elements of the culture-of-poverty myth have been used to make ideological points. Let me give an example of how this myth has been similarly used to denigrate the poor and blame them for their condition. In a November 11, 1985 column in *Newsweek*, entitled "The Soul of Conservatism," conservative commentator George Will tells us who is to blame for, and what we need to do to improve, the lot of the black poor in the United States:

One cost of bad character, and of years of condescension about "Victorian morality," is apparent in the growth of a black underclass of single-parent families in ghettos where upwards of two-thirds of all children are born out of wedlock. In the mid–1960's Pat Moynihan's report on the disintegration of black families was denounced as a racial insult. Today single-parent black families are twice as common as they were in 1965. Some scholars, who are braver than many black "leaders," argue (as Glenn Loury has in the *Public Interest*) that the principal challenge is improvement of "the values, attitudes and behaviors of individual blacks: . . . "But "society" does not cause and Congress cannot cure the calamity of sexual irresponsibility among lower-class blacks. As Kristol says, "What is wanted is a black John Wesley to do for the underclass' in the ghettos what Wesley did for the gin-ridden, loose-living working class in 18th century Britain. Reformation has to be on the agenda, not just relief."[37]

What Will has done is to take a bit of data here and a quote there, temper them in the fire on the culture-of-poverty myth, and arrive at the conclusion that the black poor are responsible for their condition and that government programs cannot and will not help. Let us look more carefully at the material Will presents and see if it merits the weight he gives it as support for the culture-of-poverty thesis.

Will tells us that single-parent black families have doubled since 1965, and he uses this as evidence of the flaw within blacks themselves. The implication is that white families have not shown such growth. If they had, then we would have to look for explanations other than weaknesses in black character. Consider, however, the data Will did not include, a comparison of the growth in single-parent families between blacks and whites for the period 1970–84, as presented in Table 2.5.

It is clear from Table 2.5 that while the proportion of single-parent families has increased for both races, these families remain much more prevalent among blacks than among whites. We must also remember, however, that poverty is a major correlate of single-parent families, and a much greater proportion of black families live in poverty than do white families. A comparison of the rate of single parenthood among poor black and poor white families will show greater

Table 2.5
Comparison of Black and White Single-Parent Households, 1970–1984 (percent)

	1970	1980	1984
Black	35.7	51.9	59.2
White	10.1	17.1	20.1

Source: U.S. Bureau of the Census, *Household and Family Characteristics* (Washington, DC: Bureau of the Census, March 1984), pp. 20, 384.

Table 2.6
Proportion of Female-Headed Families by Race and Poverty Status, 1983

	TOTAL POPULATION		NON POOR		POOR	
	Black	White	Black	White	Black	White
% FEMALE HEADED	43.1%	12.6%	29.4%	10.0%	71.5%	36.8%

Source: Characteristics of the population below the poverty level: 1983. Current Population Reports, Series P-60, #147, p. 71, February 1985. U.S. Department of Commerce, Bureau of the Census.

similarities. The proportion of female-headed families, by income and poverty status, is presented in Table 2.6. For poor families, both black and white, the proportion of female heads goes up sharply. The absolute figure remains higher for blacks, but the increment between nonpoor and poor whites is particularly telling also.

This caveat, however, is not even needed to show the fundamental error of Will's assertion that increases in black single parenthood are evidence of their inferior values. At issue in Will's assertion is the rate of increase, not the absolute levels, of single parenthood among blacks and whites. As census data in Table 2.5 show, between 1970 and 1984 the proportion of black single-parent families increased 68.5 percent (not the 100 percent argued by Will), while the proportion of white single-parent families during the same period increased 99 percent. The rate of increase in black single parenthood that Will presents as proof of black's declining morals is substantially less than the rate of increase in Will's presumed morally superior white population. Because both groups have evidenced substantial increases in the single-parent phenomenon, it makes no sense to single out black values as the cause of these increases. The movement among both groups shows either a decline in the moral values of both groups, or, more probably, the importance of other factors, such as changing economic conditions for women or changing social mores, as general causes of increasing single parenthood among all Americans.

As to Will's assertion that what blacks need is a black John Wesley to show them the way, I refer the reader to studies of the British working class of the Wesley period, studies that show a more limited reach of Wesley's ministry than Will and Kristol would have us believe. Further, this research shows the important role of the Industrial Revolution as a major impetus to modified working habits of the British poor and presents evidence that the drinking and other bad habits of the British working class persisted in spite of any change Wesley or other reformers might have wrought.[38]

What black Americans need is not a black John Wesley to help them improve weaknesses in themselves. What they need is a positive economic and social environment like that available to the British working class at the start of the Industrial Revolution in the late eighteenth and early nineteenth centuries. In twisting data and arguments to fit the culture-of-poverty bias, such conservatives as Will, Kristol, Banfield, and Sowell incorrectly interpret the nature and cause of poverty and the appropriate policies needed to soften its blows and facilitate its elimination. Throughout this chapter we have evaluated and criticized the explicit side of the conservative position on the determinants of success and failure, that is, the preeminence of values. We have seen that the culture-of-poverty thesis does not hold up to empirical scrutiny. There is, however, an implicit side to the conservative position. To argue explicitly that values are everything in achieving success or failure is to declare implicitly that environmental factors are of no significance in affecting individual and group success.

We have already seen a glimpse of the important role environmental and situational factors play in limiting and facilitating success. In Chapter 3 we will more deeply and directly look at this side of the conservative myth, the assertion that environmental and situational factors do not significantly limit or encourage individual or group success.

NOTES

1. James T. Patterson, *America's Struggle Against Poverty 1900–1980* (Cambridge, MA: Harvard University Press, 1981), p. 115.

2. William Ryan, *Blaming The Victim* (New York: Vintage Books, 1976).

3. W. Sherman Savage, *Blacks in the West* (Westport, CT: Greenwood Press, 1976), p. 14.

4. Patterson, *America's Struggle,* p. 21.

5. Chaim I. Waxman, *The Stigma of Poverty: A Critique of Poverty Theories and Policies* (New York: Pergamon Press, 1977), p. 46.

6. See, for example, Oscar Lewis's *Five Families* (New York: Basic Books, 1959); *The Children of Sanchez* (New York: Random House, 1961); and *La Vida* (New York: Random House, 1966). For a discussion of Lewis's points and for his role in the development of the culture-of-poverty theory, see Waxman, *Stigma of Poverty,* pp. 46–47;

and Charles A. Valentine, *Culture and Poverty* (Chicago: University of Chicago Press, 1968), pp. 48–77.

7. Waxman, *Stigma of Poverty,* p. 46.

8. Valentine, *Culture and Poverty,* pp. 48–63.

9. Edward C. Banfield, *The Unheavenly City* (Boston: Little, Brown, 1968).

10. Irving Kristol, *Two Cheers for Capitalism* (New York: Mentor Books, 1978).

11. George Gilder, *Wealth and Poverty* (New York: Basic Books, 1981).

12. See, for example, Sowell's *Race and Economics* (New York: David McKay, 1975); *The Economics and Politics of Race* (New York: William Morrow, 1983); or *Ethnic America* (New York: Basic Books, 1981).

13. Conservatives are not the only ideological group whose members have endorsed some element of the culture-of-poverty thesis. Some liberals and moderates also support some aspects of the myth. The focus here, however, is on conservatives because they, as a group, more deeply and more broadly embrace the elements of the myth and because they, unlike the moderate and liberal myth supporters, reject most situational caveats often associated with the thesis.

14. Examples include James Q. Wilson and Glenn Loury.

15. Examples include Irving Kristol, Charles Murray, George Gilder.

16. Banfield, *The Unheavenly City.*

17. Banfield, *The Unheavenly City,* p. 47.

18. Banfield, *The Unheavenly City,* p. 125.

19. Banfield, *The Unheavenly City,* pp. 126, 210–11.

20. Melvin L. Kohn, "Social Class and Parental Values," *American Journal of Sociology* 64 (January 1959): 337–51.

21. See National Data Program for the Social Sciences, *General Social Surveys, 1972–84: Cumulative Codebook* (National Opinion Research Center, University of Chicago, 1984).

22. Banfield, *The Unheavenly City,* p. 51.

23. Basil Bernstein, "Some Sociological Determinants of Perception," *British Journal of Sociology* 9 (June 1958): 159–74.

24. Milton Rokeach and Seymour Parker, "Values as Social Indicators of Poverty and Race Relations in America," *Annals of the American Academy of Political and Social Science* 388 (March 1970): 79–111.

25. Rokeach and Parker, "Values as Social Indicators," p. 103.

26. See any of Sowell's works.

27. Sowell, *Race and Economics,* pp. 143, 144–45, 146, 148.

28. Sowell, *Ethnic America,* p. 218. Many people, this author included, take exception to the differences Sowell asserts between U.S. and West Indian slave experiences. Debating this point, however, is really not necessary to show the flaws in Sowell's position. For a fuller picture of the U.S. slave experiences, see Herbert G. Gutman, *Slavery and the Numbers Game: A Critique of Time on the Cross* (Urbana: University of Illinois Press, 1975); Kenneth M. Stampp, *The Peculiar Institution: Slavery in the Ante-Bellum South* (New York: Vintage Books, 1956); and John W. Blassingame, *The Slave Community: Plantation Life in the Antebellum South* (New York: Oxford University Press, 1979). For a detailed discussion of West Indian slavery see Orlando Patterson, *The Sociology of Slavery: An Analysis of the Origins, Development and Structure of Negro Slave Society in Jamaica* (Rutherford, NJ: Fairleigh Dickinson University Press, 1967) (Rutherford, NJ: Fairleigh Dickinson University Press, 1967); B. W. Higman, *Slave*

Population and Economy in Jamaica, 1807–1834 (London: Cambridge University Press, 1976); and Michael Craton, *Searching for the Invisible Man: Slaves and Plantation Life in Jamaica* (Cambridge, MA: Harvard University Press, 1978).

29. Stephen Steinberg, *The Ethnic Myth* (New York: Atheneum, 1981).

30. Thomas Sowell, "Myths about Minorities," *Commentary* 68:2 (August 1979): p. 36.

31. Thomas Sowell, "Three Black Histories," in *Essays and Data on American Ethnic Groups,* ed. Thomas Sowell (Washington, DC: Urban Institute, 1978), pp. 7–64.

32. For a discussion of this formula, see N. M. Downie and R. W. Heath, *Basic Statistical Methods, 4th ed.* (New York: Harper & Row, 1974), pp. 159–63.

33. See *Census 1961, England and Wales, Birthplace and Nationality Tables,* General Registry Office (London: Her Majesty's Stationery Office, 1964); *Census 1961, England and Wales, Commonwealth Immigrants in the Conurbation,* General Registry Office (London: Her Majesty's Stationery Office, 1965); *Census 1971, Great Britain, Country of Birth Supplementary Tables Part II, Migration and Economic Activity,* Office of Population Censuses and Surveys (London: Her Majesty's Stationery Office, 1973); and *Census 1971, Great Britain, Summary Tables,* (1 percent Sample), Office of Population Censuses and Surveys (London: Her Majesty's Stationery Office, 1973).

34. Sowell, *The Economics and Politics of Race,* p. 107.

35. See, for example, Gary P. Freeman, *Immigrant Labor and Racial Conflict in Industrial Societies: The French and British Experience 1945–1975* (Princeton, NJ: Princeton University Press, 1979); and Zig Layton-Henry, *The Politics of Race in Britain* (London: George Allen & Unwin 1984).

36. Irving Kristol, "Skepticism, Meliorism, and the Public Interest," *The Public Interest* No. 81 (Fall 1985); p. 35.

37. George Will, "The Soul of Conservatism," *Newsweek,* November 11, 1985, p. 92.

38. See, for example, E. P. Thompson, *The Making of the English Working Class* (New York: Pantheon Books, 1963), pp. 350–400; G. Kitson Clark, *The Making of Victorian England* (New York: Atheneum, 1969), pp. 126–41; and Roy Porter, *English Society in the Eighteenth Century* (New York: Penguin Books, 1982), pp. 32–35, 235.

3

The Environment of Success

While conservatives and nonconservatives may disagree on the causes, there is little disagreement on the presence and persistence of significant group-based inequality in the United States. Some groups, like minorities and women, are consistently found to possess substantially less material wealth than do whites and men. As the figures in Tables 3.1 and 3.2 below indicate, group-based inequalities and the concentration of wealth in the hands of relatively few citizens have been the rule in our country for a long time.

The years 1968–85 were chosen because their data are the most current available, but past years show similar patterns. Blacks and females have had, and continue to possess, less wealth than do "dominant" groups. And while there are changes from year to year, the trend has been quite stable over the past several decades. The family income of blacks is about 60 percent of that of whites, and women's income is about 60 percent of that of men. Blacks find themselves below the poverty line at a rate three to four times that of their white fellow citizens.

At the same time that blacks and women are faring poorly vis-à-vis their white and male counterparts, the relative aggregation of wealth among various quintiles of the U.S. population shows a maldistribution of income of serious proportions. The lowest quintile of our population possesses only about 5 percent of the wealth, while the highest quintile possesses over 40 percent. And the top 5 percent of the population controls three times as much wealth as the entire bottom 20 percent of the population.

Should we be concerned about these numbers? In any free, competitive society, individuals will differ in the degree of monetary success they achieve. This is

Table 3.1
Group-Based Income Comparisons, 1968–1985

Year	Black/White Med. Family Inc. Ratio	Female/Male[a] Tot. Money Inc. Ratio	Black/White Poverty Ratio
1968	.59	.57	3.7
1970	.61	.58	3.6
1972	.58	.55	4.1
1974	.59	.58	4.0
1976	.59	.58	3.9
1978	.57	.59	4.0
1980	.58	.59	3.6
1982	.57	.61	3.0
1984	.57	.62	2.8

[a]Total money income, year around, full-time workers.

Source: Current Population Reports. Consumer Income. Series P-60,
          No. 151, 1986, p. 8, 99-100; Series P-60, No. 150, 1984, p. 7;
          Series P-60, No. 147, 1983, p. 2; and Series P-60, No. 134,
          1982, pp. 22-24.

Table 3.2
Percentage of Aggregate Income Received by Lowest Fifth, Highest Fifth, and Top 5 Percent of Families, 1968–1984

Year	% Lowest Fifth	% Highest Fifth	% Top 5%
1968	5.6	40.5	15.6
1970	5.4	40.9	15.6
1972	5.4	41.4	15.5
1974	5.5	41.0	15.5
1976	5.4	41.1	15.6
1978	5.2	41.5	15.6
1980	5.1	41.6	15.3
1982	4.7	42.7	16.0
1984	4.7	42.9	16.0

Source: Current Population Reports. Consumer Income. Series P-60,
          No. 151, April 1986, p. 37.

to be expected and even desired, given our belief that there is a strong relationship between one's effort, abilities, and productivity and one's level of monetary accomplishment. When we compare the relative monetary success of unrelated individuals whom we do not know, it is relatively easy to assume that their success, or lack thereof, is due to their ability and effort.

This comfortable belief, however, is somewhat more difficult to accept when we see whole groups or categories of individuals who share common levels of success and failure. Significant group-based differences, like the ones we have seen listed above, raise the uncomfortable possibility that systematic, non-merit-oriented factors may be at work in favor of some groups and against others.

Chapter 2 argued that a principal cornerstone of the conservative explanation for success and failure, the existence of a unique, class-based culture of poverty, is an inappropriate and incomplete explanation for the differences found in level of accomplishment across groups. This chapter will argue that another, more important factor continues to be present whenever one is faced with sorting out questions of success and failure. This is the environment in which individual and group efforts are conducted. The legal, social, economic, and political environments within which people strive have tremendous impacts on their potential and actual levels of achievement. If this is the case, then systematic, non-merit-based factors are almost certainly affecting group levels of achievement, suggesting that the proper role of the government is not to ignore the differences that result.

A major obstacle for many Americans to overcome before they accept the position of positive government action to reduce inequality is their persistent acceptance of the culture-of-poverty argument we discussed in Chapter 2. A look at survey data over the past several years indicates the pervasiveness of Americans' belief in this myth. In his pioneering work examining white attitudes toward blacks, Angus Campbell reported in a survey of citizens in 15 large, northern cities, conducted in 1968, that:

Although most of the white population has given up the belief that Negroes are inherently incapable of competing on an equal footing with whites, they have not accepted the alternative argument that Negro deficiencies are due to environmental barriers. Over half of our white respondents see the poor education, low employment status, and substandard housing of urban Negroes as due mainly to their own failure to attempt to better themselves. They appear to believe that Negroes simply lack the will to succeed as other minorities have done in preceding generations. In relying on this free-will explanation, white Americans place the whole burden of Negro disadvantage on Negroes themselves and therewith tend to deny the reality of the problems Negroes face.[1]

We are already familiar with this argument from our discussion in Chapter 2 of the position of conservative intellectuals. The poor, especially blacks, are seen as the cause of their own situation. And these explanations, given by northern whites in 1968, are still widely held today. In a Gallup survey reported in March of 1985,[2] respondents were asked, "In your opinion, which is more often to blame if a person is poor—lack of effort on his own part, or circumstances beyond his control?" The findings are reported in Table 3.3.

Nationally, over two-thirds of the sample believed that alone, or in combination with circumstances, lack of effort was responsible for a person's poverty status. Differences in perception of the causes of poverty do exist, however, across segments of the U.S. population. Women are somewhat less likely to blame lack of effort than are men. Whites are much more likely than blacks to believe, that lack of effort, not circumstance, causes poverty. And Republicans are almost twice as likely as Democrats to hold this belief.

It is clear, then, that whites and blacks see the limiting character of the

Table 3.3
Blame for Poverty

Category	Lack of Effort	Circumstances	Both	No Op.
Sex				
Males	36%	31%	30%	3%
Females	29	37	31	3
Race				
White	35	30	33	2
Black	15	67	16	2
Party ID				
Republicans	45	20	32	3
Democrats	24	48	26	2

Source: The Gallup Report, March 1985, No. 234, p. 24.

environment quite differently. This makes sense, since it is blacks who are most subject to its constraints and are, therefore, more likely to be aware of its limiting nature. Most survey data show the different ways in which the races view their situations. A 1980 Gallup survey asked blacks and whites about their quality of life.[3] Nearly twice as many whites as blacks (75 to 45 percent) felt that their quality of life had improved, while nearly five times as many blacks as whites (24 to 5 percent) felt things had gotten worse. Even though more blacks thought things had gotten better in 1980, rather than worsened, they were not nearly so positive as were whites during this period.

Another Gallup poll, taken in December of 1980,[4] asked respondents how well they thought blacks were treated in their communities. Sixty-seven percent of the whites felt blacks were treated the same as whites, but only 35 percent of the blacks felt this way. And, while only 20 percent of the whites felt blacks were treated not very well or badly, 57 percent of the blacks felt this was the case. It is clear from these findings that the races see the social and economic environment of the blacks differently. Whites see a much rosier picture for blacks than blacks do for themselves.

For many white Americans, then, individuals are responsible for their own success or failure. The environment, whether hostile or not, is merely something people with good values and skills overcome, while those with bad values and skills do not. This doctrine of a rugged individualism, impervious to environmental constraints, is strongly embraced by U.S. conservatives. It has been clearly documented by Paul Sniderman of Stanford University in his *Race and Inequality: A Study in American Values.*[5] In a 1972 national survey, Sniderman used respondent answers to six questions about the causes of racial inequality to divide Americans into four types: individualists, progressives, fundamentalists, and historicists. Individualists were those who agreed with the statement that blacks were a less able race and disagreed with the statement that powerful external forces control things and act to keep blacks down.

The first thing Sniderman discovered was that over half of those surveyed could be classified as individualists (56 percent). Even more important to the present discussion, he found that individualists were also the most conservative among the four types:

Individualists are clearly conservative; only they are on the right, politically and graphically, on the issue of government guarantees for jobs and standard of living. The same goes for the issue of law and order; forced to choose between protecting the rights of those accused of crime and stopping crime, only the individualists are to the right of the average. The problem of urban riots reflects another facet of this law-and-order stance; here, too, the position of the individualists is distinctively conservative. They are also on the political right with respect to government programs for blacks and other minorities. . . . And not only do individualists take conservative positions; they think of themselves as conservative.[6]

It is very clear, then, that a substantial number of Americans embrace the individualist perspective on success and that this group is much more conservative than are other groups of Americans. The important question is, is this belief correct? While many may embrace this position, it represents a very incomplete explanation of success and failure. The analysis of the legal, political, social, and economic factors presented in this chapter will show that environmental factors can and do facilitate the success of some and limit the success of others. U.S. conservatives to the contrary, the environment is much more than a neutral presence; it is an active force molding and limiting the efforts of individuals and groups. An explication of the structural and attitudinal factors that have helped some and impeded others lies at the heart of any government's response to the inequalities it sees in its population.

THE CORRELATES OF INEQUALITY

Economists have done some of the more detailed inquiries into the nature of income inequality in the United States. In study after study, economists, using multiple-regression techniques, have identified the factors that explain income differentials among the populace. And the consistency of these studies is relatively remarkable, with different researchers identifying similar correlates and explaining similar amounts of variation in income inequality.[7] What economists have discovered is that education, race, sex, geographic location, and family-background characteristics, such as father's occupation and education, have strong individual relationships with income inequality and, when taken together, explain about 30–50 percent of all the variance in income inequality.

Most economists feel that a complicated, microanalytic model, like those used to explain income inequality, is doing very well if it can explain 30–50 percent of the variance. They do acknowledge, however, that their models are not perfect and that much of the variation in inequality remains unexplained. There are two interpretations of this unexplained variance. One is that it is simply measurement error resulting from the general problem of explaining complex, individual-level social phenomena with imperfect measures. The second is that the unexplained variance captures the discrimination within the market itself; that is, that the market is only partially driven by neutral, nondiscriminatory, "rational" factors and that the rest of the inequality observed is due to active market discrimination.

Both of these explanations are probably correct. Some of the unexplained variance is most certainly due to measurement problems; but there is also likely to be some discrimination occurring as well. This latter assertion is supported by econometric extrapolations of what blacks and women would be likely to earn if they had the same background characteristics as white males. Assuming equal resources, researchers still find blacks and women making less than their white male counterparts, although the gap does close substantially.[8] For most economists, however, this closing of the gap is viewed as proof that the market is working correctly and rewarding merit, and, if blacks and women had the appropriate premarket characteristics, they would be doing better.

For many economists, then, the findings of their econometric analyses of income inequality are neither unusual nor controversial. In a market economy, they would argue, one expects different backgrounds, abilities, and motivational levels, what economists call "human capital," to produce different incomes. The surprise would be if this were not the case. These economists accept as given the particular array of human-capital resources different individuals and groups bring to the market competition. They are generally not concerned with how some individuals or groups obtained the relative level of human capital that makes them more or less successful in the market competition they face.

How premarket forces affect the human-capital acquisition opportunities of various groups is at the very heart of understanding the nature of income inequality in the United States. Why does one group bring more human-capital resources to the competition than does another? This is a crucial question, because those who have had the opportunity to acquire greater amounts of human capital will be more successful in the competition that lies ahead. If this acquisition process is uneven or unfair, if some are facilitated in acquiring capital, while others are discouraged or blocked, then the outcomes of the competition, and the inequalities that result, cannot be accepted simply as the natural results of a fair, competitive, nondiscriminatory market process.

The diagram below, developed by economist Lars Osberg, may help us to understand better the complex market and premarket forces and their interplay in affecting income inequalities (Figure 3.1). Osberg arrays the variables economists have found to be correlated with income levels, and in his presentation we can clearly see the important current human-capital resources of our competitors (age, education, intelligence, health, drive and aspirations, and so on),

Figure 3.1
Influences on Individual Earnings

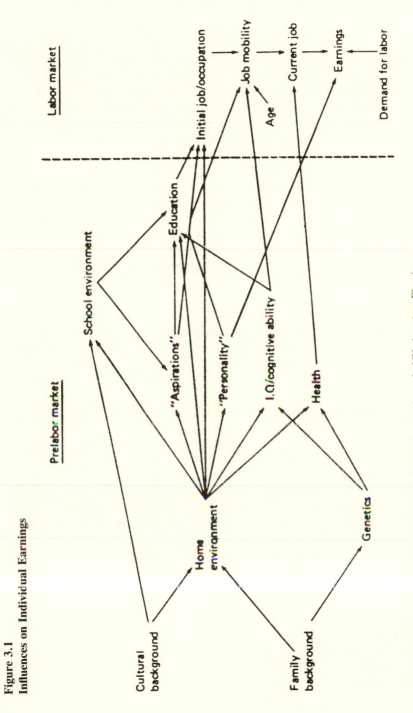

Source: Lars Osberg, *Economic Inequality in the United States*, (Armonk, NY: American Elsevier, 1984), p. 188. Reprinted with permission.

but we can also see the importance of precursor variables (family, home environment, school environment, and so forth). These background factors have an indirect impact on earnings through the various individual-level human-capital variables. It is a multistep process: Family background variables, the home environment, and the school environment affect education level, cognitive ability, and health and personality variables, which, in turn, directly relate to the job and earnings variables. If something discriminatory is going on at the pre-market competition phase to limit the ability of certain groups to develop their human-capital resources, then the resulting job and earnings inequalities will be affected, however discriminatory or nondiscriminatory the particular present-day employer–employee job market.

Since economists have shown us the importance of family background variables, especially father's occupation and education, in the determintion of income inequality, we can now see the discriminatory acts that in the past may have limited your father's opportunities will likely have a limiting effect on your capital development and may result in your achieving less in the market competition. If past discriminatory actions, either by governments, businesses, or individuals, acted to limit the advancement of your parents or grandparents, you will be limited in the acquisition of the human capital needed to compete for income.

The inescapable fact is that just such premarket discrimination has acted to hold down the development of human-capital resources among black Americans. In the pages that follow, I will outline the legal and attitudinal factors that have systematically acted to prevent American blacks from accumulating the human and fiscal capital they need to be successful economically in the United States.

THE SOUTH AND JIM CROW

Only 70 years ago, near the turn of the century, 90 percent of black Americans lived in the South.[9] The overwhelming majority of black men and women living today had fathers and grandfathers who came of age in a region of our country that systematically denied them basic social, economic, and political opportunities. The ubiquitous Jim Crow or segregation laws that grew out of the post-Civil War and Reconstruction experience of southern states acted to profoundly limit the fiscal and human-capital potential of the black citizens living under its rule. Not until the 1950s did some of these legal restrictions come under attack and southern blacks had to wait until the late 1960s and early 1970s before systematic state-based discrimination against them was limited by national laws and court decisions. As recently as 15 years ago southern blacks had to face serious legal restrictions in their search for educational, economic, and political opportunities.

Segregation and its concomitant inferior commitment to black education, political participation, housing, and economic development are recorded in history and are not disputed.[10] What is surprising is that many today, particularly conservatives, do not view this profound experience as limiting the opportunities of the offspring of the blacks subjected to this active discrimination. Economists should be the first to tell them that, since family characteristics are so important in determining offspring human-capital resources, actions that limited the human-capital (and fiscal-capital) development of black fathers and grandfathers must limit the opportunities of their offspring. And it is not as if these limits occurred so long ago as to be irrelevant today. For most, the limits are only one or two generations away.

The link between past discrimination, which no one would deny, and present-day income inequality is illustrated plainly in the work of the econometricians. Premarket factors, particularly family characteristics and accomplishments, which had been severely restricted for years for black Americans, are inextricably related to market success.

WHITES' ATTITUDES TOWARD BLACKS

In addition to the rather substantial legal barriers that black Americans have had to face, other equally important barriers have prevented them from fully developing their fiscal- and human-capital resources. These are the negative attitudes white citizens have held about blacks, attitudes that led to the support of restrictive laws, to segregated and inferior education, housing, and public accommodations, to discrimination in hiring and promotions, to social ostracism, and ultimately to decreased opportunities to develop the fiscal- and human-capital resources needed to succeed economically in this country.

The interesting and disturbing fact is that these attitudes have never been hidden and have been known for a long time. Survey research studies since the 1920s have documented the negative view many white Americans have held of their black fellow citizens. Beginning in 1924, noted sociologist Emory Bogardus began looking at the "social distance" between whites and blacks in this country. Social distance is defined as the extent to which one group likes and feels itself similar to another group. Bogardus developed a scale to measure these feelings by asking respondents to agree or disagree with a set of seven statements about the members of other groups: would marry, would have as regular friends, would work beside in an office, would have several families in the neighborhood, would have merely as speaking acquaintances, would have live outside the neighborhood, and would have live outside the country.[11] Table 3.4 summarizes Bogardus's social-distance findings for 30 ethnic groups over the past several decades.

What Bogardus's studies show is that blacks have been viewed in a very negative way both absolutely and in comparison to other ethnic groups in our country. Out of 30 groups examined, blacks were 26th with a score of 3.28 in 1926, 29th with a score of 3.60 in 1946, 27th with a score of 2.74 in 1956, and 29th with a score of 2.56 in 1966. Blacks consistently are ranked at or near the bottom in every study. Compared with other ethnic groups in the United States blacks have a uniquely negative position, which has persisted for years. And

Table 3.4
Social Distance by Scores and Ranks for Ethnic Groups, 1926–1966

	1926		1946		1956		1968	
1.	English	1.06	Americans	1.04	Americans	1.08	Americans	1.07
2.	Americans	1.10	Canadians	1.11	Canadians	1.16	English	1.14
3.	Canadians	1.13	English	1.13	English	1.23	Canadians	1.15
4.	Scots	1.13	Irish	1.24	French	1.47	French	1.36
5.	Irish	1.30	Scots	1.26	Irish	1.56	Irish	1.40
6.	French	1.32	French	1.31	Swedish	1.57	Swedish	1.42
7.	Germans	1.46	Norwegians	1.35	Scots	1.60	Norwegians	1.50
8.	Swedish	1.54	Hollanders	1.37	Germans	1.61	Italians	1.51
9.	Hollanders	1.56	Swedish	1.40	Hollanders	1.63	Scots	1.53
10.	Norwegians	1.59	Germans	1.59	Norwegians	1.66	Germans	1.54
11.	Spanish	1.72	Finns	1.63	Finns	1.80	Hollanders	1.54
12.	Finns	1.83	Czechs	1.76	Italians	1.89	Finns	1.67
13.	Russians	1.88	Russians	1.83	Poles	2.07	Greeks	1.82
14.	Italians	1.94	Poles	1.84	Spanish	2.08	Spanish	1.93
15.	Poles	2.01	Spanish	1.94	Greeks	2.09	Jews	1.97
16.	Armenians	2.06	Italians	2.28	Jews	2.15	Poles	1.98
17.	Czechs	2.08	Armenians	2.29	Czechs	2.22	Czechs	2.02

#	Group	Score	#	Group	Score	#	Group	Score	#	Group	Score
18.	Indians A	2.38	18.	Greeks	2.29	18.	Armenians	2.33	18.	Indians A	2.12
19.	Jews	2.39	19.	Jews	2.32	19.	Japanese A	2.34	19.	Japanese A	2.14
20.	Greeks	2.47	20.	Indians A	2.45	20.	Indians A	2.35	20.	Armenians	2.18
21.	Mexicans	2.69	21.	Chinese	2.50	21.	Filipinos	2.46	21.	Filipinos	2.31
22.	Mexican A	----	22.	Mexican A	2.52	22.	Mexican A	2.51	22.	Chinese	2.34
23.	Japanese	2.80	23.	Filipinos	2.76	23.	Turks	2.52	23.	Mexican A	2.37
24.	Japanese A	----	24.	Mexicans	2.89	24.	Russians	2.56	24.	Russians	2.38
25.	Filipinos	3.00	25.	Turks	2.89	25.	Chinese	2.68	25.	Japanese	2.41
26.	Negroes	3.28	26.	Japanese A	2.90	26.	Japanese	2.70	26.	Turks	2.48
27.	Turks	3.30	27.	Koreans	3.05	27.	Negroes	2.74	27.	Koreans	2.51
28.	Chinese	3.36	28.	Indians I	3.43	28.	Mexicans	2.79	28.	Mexicans	2.56
29.	Koreans	3.60	29.	Negroes	3.60	29.	Indians I	2.80	29.	Negroes	2.56
30.	Indians I	3.91	30.	Japanese	3.61	30.	Koreans	2.83	30.	Indians I	2.62

Social distance scores can vary from 1 to 7, with 7 being the most negative, or distant.

Source: C. A. Owen, H. C. Eisner, and T. R. McFaul, "A Half-Century of Social Distance Research: National Replication of the Bogardus' Studies," *Sociology and Social Research* 66 (1) (October 1981): 84.

Table 3.5
White Attitudes toward Blacks, Selected Items, 1942–1983 (percent supporting)

Year	Same Schools[1]	Equal Nhbr[1]	Same Trans.[1]	Hire Equally[1]	Inter-Marriage[2]
1942	30%	35%	44%	--	--
1944	--	--	--	42	--
1946	--	--	--	47	--
1956	49	52	60	--	--
1963	62	65	77	83	--
1968	--	--	--	--	20
1970	74	76	88	--	--
1972	85	84	--	96	29
1978	--	--	--	--	36
1983	--	--	--	--	--

[1]Source: T. W. Smith and P. B. Sheatsley, "American Attitudes Toward Race Relations," *Public Opinion*, October/November 1984, p. 15.

[2]Source: Gallup Report #213, June 1983, p. 10.

while the level of distance has decreased somewhat in the 1956 and 1966 studies, the relative position of blacks has remained consistently low.

Similar negative attitudes about blacks have also been recorded for more nationally based samples examined since 1942. Table 3.5 shows the results of national surveys examining white attitudes toward joint school attendance, having an "equal" black neighbor, riding the same streetcar or bus, job-hiring chances, and intermarriage. Significant negative positions vis-à-vis blacks existed before the 1960s, although some of these attitudes have changed markedly since the civil rights revolution of the mid–1960s. What is important for this analysis is that, like Bogardus's students, national samples showed consistent negative orientations toward blacks, especially in the pre–1960 period, a period that is crucial to today's blacks in terms of the development of their fathers' and their own human-capital resources.

And there are other indicators that illustrate the environmental problem blacks face because of the attitudinal positions of white Americans. A simple but telling example is the extent to which Americans report their willingness to support a black for president of the United States. Gallup has chronicled Americans' support for this proposition since 1958, and the figures are reported in Table 3.6. While the trend indicates less hostility toward the idea of a black president, the substantial opposition, especially in the pre-civil-rights legislation period, indicates significant hostility to America's blacks. (And remember, these samples include blacks, so the levels of white support are actually lower than these numbers imply.) Here is a basic American dream—that any of us can grow up to become president—denied for years to America's black citizens.

Why should we care about this negative attitudinal environment within which American blacks have had to function for the past 100 years? It is important because, as social scientists have consistently demonstrated, attitudes influence

Table 3.6
Vote for Black for President, 1958–1983

Year	%Yes	%No	%No Opinion
1958	38	53	9
1963	47	45	8
1965	59	34	7
1967	54	40	6
1969	67	23	10
1971	70	23	7
1978	77	18	5
1983	77	16	7

Source: Gallup Report #212, May, 1983, p. 18.

behavior. Negative attitudes toward blacks, therefore, will almost inevitably lead to negative behaviors toward blacks, behaviors that limit blacks' opportunities to succeed. Most of the evaluation decisions made by whites in their capacities as employers, teachers, service deliverers, and so on had a significant subjective component. And the historical evidence is compelling that the degrees of freedom available to many of these whites, especially southern ones, were hardly likely to be used to benefit blacks. Even if things are improving now, the damage to current competitors is already done.

Although public and private enterprises now try to develop objective measures of performance and ability on which to make success-related choices among competitors, few attempts were made to objectify such decisions before 1965. And even now the fact is that accurate and objective evaluations of ability are inadequate and rudimentary at best, leaving a substantial portion of any evaluation still subjective in nature. Those who belonged to groups that were less positively viewed (as the social distance and attitudinal studies show that blacks were) suffered in these subjective considerations and were less likely to be rewarded for their efforts. Being properly rewarded for effort is important not only for achieving what one deserves in a particular competition; it is important for how it affects one's view of self and one's potential for future success-oriented behaviors.

BLACK SELF-CONCEPT

We have discussed the direct impact that negative legal and attitudinal environments can have on opportunities for blacks to develop the human-capital resources they need to be successful. There is also a strong and insidious indirect consequence of these two negative forces for lack of black success. This is the fact that striving hard in a relatively unrewarding environment may create beliefs and attitudes in blacks about the likelihood of failure that discourage them from continuing to try to achieve.

Psychologists tell us that for appropriate behaviors to be learned, individuals' actions must receive relatively consistent consequences. In their terminology, psychologists argue that behaviors must have appropriate contingencies, if they are to be maintained. If behavior X is supposed to result in a reward, then if I perform behavior X, I should get rewarded. If everything works this way, the behavior is said to have the proper contingencies. Things go awry when consequences of particular behaviors are not contingent, where behaviors have little guarantee that they will achieve any given results.[12]

Seligman has argued that when individuals have repeated experiences where outcomes are noncontingent, that is, where rewards or punishments are perceived to be unrelated to what is done, it can lead to a state of "learned helplessness."[13] Seligman's position is a simple and compelling one: An individual notices that whatever he does, however well and however hard he tries, nothing positive seems to come of it. This can be learned early and in a particular situation—let us call it situation X. Even when situation X is over, the individual may generalize the learned helplessness to other, less appropriate situations. This generalization thereby limits attempts at appropriate behaviors that might lead to success in the new situation.

The old situation is gone and with hard work, one might now succeed, but the effort is not made because of the pattern developed earlier. Remember, early learned behavioral patterns may persist, even when the situation which they develop may no longer be present. Therefore, early noncontingent experiences may lead to the development of a learned-helplessness pattern of behavior, which generalizes to a lack of task persistence even though there is a new, more favorable environment.

Seligman's position is echoed by other psychologists, who may use other concepts, in addition to helplessness, to explain this set of relationships. These related concepts include locus of control[14] and attribution,[15] but the fundamental argument is the same. People respond to their environments. Hostile, substantially noncontingent environments may lead to negative perceptions of self and to limited attempts to succeed. When we see the members of certain groups trying less to succeed, it may have little or nothing to do with fundamental values or any culture of poverty, but rather with very real and not totally inappropriate responses to an often correctly perceived hostile environment.[16]

People are not born with negative or positive self-images; they must learn them. People are not born with positive attitudes toward work or success or striving hard to achieve. These must also be learned. The middle and upper classes work in an arena of relatively well understood contingencies. They learn that they are good, worthy, and have a great chance of success. The poor, on the other hand, have existed in an arena of relatively imperfect contingencies. What they often learn from their environment is that they are bad, unworthy, and unlikely to succeed, however hard they try. As we view our real environments, we develop expectations of our chances of success from the examples we see and from our own experiences. Problems occur if our own experiences and the experiences of our models result in adaptations that are negative from the dominant culture's perspective and unlikely to enable achievement under that culture's rules.

People living in poverty who work hard and are dependable may still get nowhere, while the pimps and drug dealers "succeed." The latter path is wrong and deviant to us because we use our experience and our array of choices to evaluate its relevance. For the poverty group that path may seem to be a more appropriate—or at least less inappropriate—one, given the real environment they face or perceive.

This discussion of adaptive and reactive attitudes and beliefs should not be confused with the cultural values discussion presented in Chapter 2. The concepts are quite distinct. Values refer to the fundamental orientations and goals of people, while beliefs and attitudes refer to orientations to a given environmental context. Turner and Starnes have made this distinction very clear:

Values are those highly general and abstract conceptions that are held by members of a population and that provide the criteria for defining and assessing desirable conduct. As such, values provide the standards by which members of a population evaluate their own conduct and that of others. Although these standards often guide and regulate behavior and are therefore an important source of social control in social systems, many other forces shape human action. . . .

Beliefs are concrete conceptions that are held by members of a population and that reveal their understandings about what exists in particular settings and their feelings about what the state of affairs should be in a particular setting. As such, two general types of beliefs can be discerned: (1) *evaluative beliefs* pertaining to concrete conceptions of what should exist in a specified setting; and *empirical beliefs* referring to concrete concepts about what actually exists in a particular setting.[17] (emphasis in original)

It is not inconsistent, therefore, to argue in Chapter 2 that the poor share basic cultural values relating to success, while also arguing that in specific, negative environmental contexts, these same individuals may hold rather negative attitudes and beliefs about their actual chances of success. The poor, then, do not have a different set of cultural values; they have a different perception of their likelihood of success, based on their often accurate view of the negative environment they face. And these adaptive attitudes and beliefs may lead to behaviors that do not help them break out of their negative situation.

THE INHERITANCE OF ADVANTAGE

We have already seen how the environment can limit opportunities for some individuals and groups, to the obvious advantage of their competitors. This same environment also bestows significant advantages to the progeny of the advantaged groups. The principal vehicle through which benefits are passed from one group of haves to another is inheritance. Many types of fiscal and human capital can be and are passed on from one generation to the next. The poor, disadvantaged, and discriminated-against receive a triple whammy. Not only are they limited by the failure of their ancestors to accumulate assets and by the negative environments they themselves face in attempting to accrue assets, but their children will suffer a similar fate, because current competitors will not accumulte fiscal- or human-capital assets to pass on to them. Here is the true cycle of poverty.

Conservatives want us to believe that the rich have achieved their exalted status through hard work, ability, and merit. Reality does not match this belief, however. The econometricians discussed above have already demonstrated the importance of family background in affecting current levels of income achievement. These economists are not referring to the transmission of fiscal assets from family to offspring, by rather, the transmission of genetic ability, positive home and educational environment, a positive attitude about work and the chance for success, and so on. These are the human-capital assets that one group of successful people passes on to their children.

And while these "inherited" human-capital assets are important, especially for the middle classes, for the upper classes they may be much less important sources of wealth than the actual transmission of fiscal assets. By transmission of fiscal assets is meant not only the monetary inheritance that occurs after the death of a parent. Transmission of fiscal assets includes this type of transfer, but also the gifts, loans, business positions, fiancial contacts, and other tangible fiscal benefits upper-class parents can bestow on their children.

The fact is that substantial accumulations of wealth are transferred from one generation to the next through these mechanisms. Since we are all familiar with the passage of wealth via inheritance at death, let us look at this mechanism first. Our first impression, and a correct one, is that it is a powerful, non-merit-based vehicle for transferring wealth from one person to another, for people on the receiving end of the transfer are not particularly more able or more meritorious than anyone else. They are simply the relatives of wealthy people.

Scientific studies and popular investigations have demonstrated the importance of inheritance of wealth due to the demise of someone else. In a detailed investigation of the intergenerational transfer of wealth among the wealthiest families in Great Britain, Josiah Wedgewood found that "in the great majority of cases, the large fortunes of one generation belong to the children of those who possessed the large fortunes of the preceding generations."[18] More popular investigations of this question, such as that done by *Forbes* and *Fortune* magazines, report similar findings. For example, well over 50 percent of the *Forbes 400* wealthiest individuals are listed as inheritors of their wealth.[19]

This percentage may be artificially low in estimating the true benefit one receives from wealthy relatives or friends, since it focuses on asset transfer at death only. John Brittain has commented on the substantial advantages the wealthy may bestow on their offspring without any formal asset transfer at death and the difficulty in truly capturing all the benefit one receives both from this type of transfer and from actual asset transfer at death:

The *Fortune* surveys concluded that only half of the ultra rich achieved their wealth via inheritance. . . . But the *Fortune* classification of the wealthy into two categories—inherited and self-made—may be misleading. For example, J. Paul Getty's fortune was put at $700 million to $1 billion in 1957 when he was 65 years old, and it was not classified as inherited. Yet Getty is reported to have inherited one-half million dollars; perhaps more important, he has described how his early wildcatting ventures were fully financed by his father, as some kind of silent partner. An appraisal of the extent to which his 1957 fortune was inherited requires knowledge of the timing of these transfers from his father, what he already had when they were received, and Getty's own long-run rate of return on his capital. For example, if he put up none of the original investment and earned only an average rate of return, the entire fortune should be regarded as inherited. Of course, if he earned an extraordinary rate of return, it would seem reasonable to credit him with some independent accumulation even if he put up nothing. In any case, only careful analysis could tell whether or not his inheritance and earlier financial backing was of primary importance in the building of Getty's fortune.[20]

The inescapable fact, as the Getty example demonstrates, is that the true assistance parents provide their offspring goes far beyond simple transfers of assets at death. Any detailed investigation of the full range of this assistance will show that the role of inheritance in wealth accumulation is even greater than the significant proportions found in existing studies. As Brittain has made clear,"it is apparent that the impact of [a father's] wealth is transmitted to sons via environmental advantages, education provided, and other channels—not via financial transfers alone."[21] There may be many fewer self-made men than conservatives imagine.

So far we have focused on the intergenerational transfer of wealth among the very wealthy. It is possible for one to argue that while inheritance may be significant for this group, for the rest of us it has little impact on our level of economic accomplishments. Some economists, however, have directly measured the role of inheritance, of family position, on economic accomplishment and have found its impact to be profound. In an important study Brittain found that brothers showed a strong tendency to achieve similar status.[22] In fact, Brittain found "between 34 and 67 percent of the variance of economic status explained by family effects."[23] And these are everyday citizens, not a wealthy subsample.

In another totally unrelated study, Paul Taubman examined the economic accomplishments of a sample of twins and also found a tremendous overlap in the economic status of both pair members.[24] In his sample Taubman found that similar family origins account for between 30 and 55 percent of the total variance in twins' earnings.[25] Considering all aspects of family contribution, the clear importance of family in affecting individual earning potential led Taubman to conclude that "given the environmental variation that existed in the cohort under study, a substantial portion of the variance in earnings was determined prior to entry into the labor market, . . . a large portion of the total variance (in individual earnings) was determined very early and the effects of individual effort appear to be more limited than I would like to believe."[26]

What we have seen in Brittain's and Taubman's analyses of brother pairs is the tremendous impact family has in influencing individuals' incomes. Much as conservatives might like to believe that individual merit alone determines wealth, the facts indicate that what one starts with, the fiscal- and human-capital resources one receives from one's family, has a great deal to do with levels of achievement. The class position of children is, to an extent that conservatives will find quite uncomfortable, greatly influenced by their current family class position. As Brittain has shown;

We can compare the predicted family incomes of sons with advantageous background to those of sons who are less fortunate. Adjusting the incomes to a 1976 basis, a son who ranks 10 percent from the top in background is predicted to have an income of $25,200, while his opposite number with background rank 10 percent from the bottom has a predicted income of $11,500—less than half that predicted for the advantaged son. For sons with background ranks in the middle of the top and bottom 5 percent, respectively, the predictions are $30,900 and $9,400. Even more striking than these differentials are the chances of a son's earning a given income or higher. Consider the same two contrasts in background rank specified above. The estimate . . . is that the son ranking 10 percent from the top in background had a 51 percent chance of having a 1976 family income of $25,000 or more, compared to a 2 percent chance for his disadvantaged opposite number.[27]

The degree of intergenerational mobility across classes is an issue of extreme importance in the debate about the sources of wealth in the United States. If, as these studies indicate, there is relatively little intergenerational mobility across classes, if the children of the rich are also rich and if the children of the poor are also poor, then the conservative homily about the importance of merit as the arbiter of wealth rings very hollow indeed.

But what about class mobility within a given generation? Even though the studies presented above show the tremendous importance of family past in determining current wealth, these transmissions are not perfect. It is absolutely true that some who begin with silver spoons in their mouths live to see them tarnished, and surely some who begin with little are able to accumulate more than their families could. The important questions for us to consider are how many experience these deviations, how far is their resultant rise or fall, and what causes this movement.

To investigate this question we need to examine, over time, the income and class fluctuations of particular families and individuals. In a fixed period of time, do these individuals and families show class mobility and if so, how much and for what reasons? In one of the most ambitious social science investigations of its kind, a research team at the University of Michigan, led by Greg Duncan, has performed such a study. Calling it The Panel Study of Income Dynamics, Duncan and his colleagues examined the economic trends in 5,000 families from 1967 to 1978. What these investigators found is pretty much what we would

Table 3.7

Estimated Fractions of the U.S. Population in Various Combinations of 1971 and 1978 Family Income Quintiles

Family Income Quintile in 1971	Family Income Quintile in 1978					
	Lowest	Fourth	Third	Second	Highest	All
Lowest	11.1%	4.4%	1.9%	1.4%	1.2%	20.0%
Fourth	4.3	6.9	4.3	2.7	1.8	20.0
Third	2.7	4.7	6.1	3.7	2.8	20.0
Second	1.2	3.0	5.1	6.3	4.4	20.0
Highest	0.7	0.9	2.8	5.9	9.7	20.0
All	20.0%	19.9%	20.2%	20.0%	19.9%	100.0%

Table reads: "Of all individuals in 1971, 20.0% lived in families whose incomes placed them in the lowest income quintile, but just 11.1% of all individuals placed in the lowest quintile in both 1971 and 1978. The other 8.9% had moved upward to the fourth (4.4%), third (1.9%), second (1.4%), or highest (1.2%) quintiles."

Source: Greg J. Duncan and James N. Morgan, "An Overview of Family Economic Mobility," in Greg J. Duncan et al., Years of Poverty, Years of Plenty (Ann Arbor, MI: Institute for Social Research, The University of Michigan, 1984), p. 10 & 13. Reprinted by permission of the Institute for Social Research.

have expected from the other studies reported above. In the economic evolution of these families one finds both stability and movement. Reproduced in Table 3.7 are the summary mobility findings Duncan and his colleagues report in their multiyear effort, *Years of Poverty, Years of Plenty.*[28]

Looking at this table is like looking at a glass half-filled with water. For some, the glass is half-full, for others the glass is half-empty. For American conservatives, the glass is clearly half-full. Each quintile shows movement both up and down the class scale. For the lowest quintile, nearly half moved into a higher category, while for the highest quintile, more than half moved downward.

Critics of the conservative position see the glass half-empty. Most of the people in a given quintile in 1971 were still there in 1978. And while there clearly is movement across quintiles, both up and down, the movement is largely limited to only one quintile. Most of those in the lowest quintile who experienced upward mobility moved only to the next lowest quintile, while the overwhelming majority of those in the highest quintile moved only to the next highest one.

It may help both sides interpret what they see if we can identify the sources of this movement, both up and down. Is it merit based, as conservatives believe, the result of harder work and greater effort among some individuals? Or is it structurally based, the result of less merit-oriented processes such as aging or family structural rearrangements? Duncan's own interpretation of his findings may shed some light on this controversy:

When we compare the economic position of the population in two years, 1971 and 1978, we find a remarkable amount of change at all income levels. Of those who were either at the top or at the bottom levels in 1971, only about half had remained in those relative positions in 1978. More surprising, a look at growth in economic status over time shows that a majority managed to keep their incomes growing faster than inflation despite the rapid inflation and severe recession. Next, when we examine our data more closely, we find that neither differences in the personality traits or skills of the family members nor events such as unemployment or disability can account well for these widespread changes. Instead, we find that the single most important factor accounting for changes in family well-being was a fundamental change in family structure: divorce, death, marriage, birth, or a child leaving home. In other words, changes in the economic status of families are linked inextricably to changes in the composition of families themselves. Indeed, the variety and frequency of observed family composition changes are great enough to make the very concept of "family" ambiguous when placed in a dynamic context. Adding to a growing body of evidence about the economic importance of the family, these findings suggest that individuals may have more control over their economic status through decisions about marriage, divorce, procreation, or sharing households with relatives or friends, than they do about seeking more work or better-paying jobs.[29]

What the Michigan panel study and the intergenerational analyses make clear is that there is very little *merit-based* economic mobility in the United States. Most get all or a large part of what they start with directly or indirectly from their parents, and if they move up or down, the causes are much more likely to be structural than merit-based in nature.

CONCLUSION

Black Americans have faced a significantly hostile legal, political, and social environment, an environment substantially more hostile than that encountered by any other ethnic group in the United States. And although this negative environment is improving, the damage done to the aspirations and actual fiscal- and human-capital acquisition by past and current generations of blacks is profound.

Conservatives have tried to console themselves about this sad state of affairs with the argument that other ethnic groups, like the Irish, Italians, or Jews, faced similar hostility, and in only two or three generations they succeeded. If blacks have not, it is their own fault. What we have seen presented in this chapter is that the assertion that blacks and these other ethnic group faced similar negative environments is absolutely unsupportable.

While most of the Irish, Italian, and Jewish ethnics were living in the North or Midwest at the turn of the century, black Americans were residing in the South. While no one would deny the hostility faced by Irish, Italian, and Jews in the non-South, to compare it to the systematic legal oppression and ostracism of the blacks in the South is an error of significant proportions. Few things can more clearly point out the profundity of these differences than the levels of

Table 3.8
Lynchings, by Region and Race, 1904–1927

Region and Race	N	%
Southern Blacks	1,227	78
Southern Whites	100	6
Border-state Blacks	125	6
Border-state Whites	28	3
All Other Blacks	34	3
All Other Whites	33	3
TOTALS	1,547	100

Source: Gerald M. Pomper, Elections in America (2nd ed.), p. 189.

violence blacks experienced compared to whites in the crucial years following the turn of the century. Table 3.8 presents data on lynching, by race and region, for the years 1904–27. The higher proportions of violent acts directed against blacks compared to whites illustrates the completely different character and seriousness of the environments that were faced by northern white ethnics and southern blacks. Without denigrating the accomplishments of white ethnic groups, which was substantial, figures like these point out the profound differences in the legal and attitudinal restrictions and hostility black southerners faced.

The white ethnics attended the same schools, exercised the same political freedoms, purchased the same housing (with a few exceptions), visited the same public accommodations, and joined the same unions as did their Anglo-Saxon neighbors. This was hardly the case for black southerners. And as our social-distance comparisons indicate, the level of attitudinal hostility faced by blacks for most of this century was substantially greater than that encountered by the white ethnics the conservatives hold up as their success models.

And finally, there is the question of time. Conservatives tell us of the success in two to three generations accomplished by the white ethnics. Where is the comparable black success, they ask? In addition to the above points, another important answer is that for many generations of blacks, the restrictions holding down their opportunities to develop fiscal and human capital were struck down just 15 years ago in the series of civil-rights legislation and Supreme Court decisions of the 1960s and 1970s. Not even one generation free of the serious constraints of discriminatory laws and attitudes has had a chance to mature. And remember, even they will be limited by the lack of fiscal- and human-capital resources their parents will be able to pass on to them and by the learned helplessness of generations without hope—a learned helplessness not experienced by the white ethnics who could see the fruits of their efforts almost immediately.

NOTES

1. Angus Cambell, *White Attitudes Toward Black People* (Ann Arbor: Institute for Social Research, The University of Michigan, 1971), pp. 41–42.
2. *Gallup Report* #234, March 1985, p. 24.
3. *Gallup Report* #178, June 1980, p. 10.
4. *Gallup Report* #185, February 1981, p. 35.
5. Paul M. Sniderman; *Race and Inequality: A Study in American Values* (Chatham, NJ: Chatham House, 1985).
6. Sniderman, *Race and Inequality,* p. 51.
7. See, for example, Lars Osberg; *Economic Inequality in the United States* (Armonk, NY: Sharpe, 1984); Paul Taubman; *Sources of Inequality in Earnings* (New York: American Elsevier), and Barry R. Chiswick, *Income Inequality* (New York: National Bureau of Economic Research, 1974). For a comprehensive review of the income inequality literature, see Gian Singh Sahota, "Theories of Personal Income Distribution: A Survey," *Journal of Economic Literature* 16 (March 1978): 1–55. For a somewhat contrary position see Christoper Jencks, *Inequality* (New York: Harper & Row, 1973).
8. For a review of these findings, see R. J. Flanagan, R. S. Smith, and R. G. Ehrenberg; *Labor Economics and Labor Relations* (Glenview, IL: Scott, Foresman, 1984), pp. 292–94.
9. The southern black experience is emphasized in this section because at the time U.S. northern white ethnics were beginning their successful struggle in the large cities of the North and Midwest, most American blacks were living in the South. While it is true that the experiences of significant numbers of these southern blacks who flocked to the cities of the North and Midwest between the two world wars was relatively less negative than that faced by their southern brothers and sisters, the presentations in this chapter and Chapter 4 will show that they, too, found a more hostile set of attitudes and social and political structures than did white ethnics living in the same areas.
10. Specific programs and patterns of segregation and discrimination in education, political participation, public accommodations, and government services will be presented in Chapter 4.
11. For a discussion of Bogardus's approach, see C. A. Owen, H. C. Eisner, and T. R. McFaul, "A Half-Century of Social Distance Research: National Replication of the Bogardus' Studies," *Sociology and Social Research* 66 (October 1981): 80–98.
12. For a discussion of the importance of contingency-based learning, see Steve Worchel and Joel Cooper, *Understanding Social Psychology,* 3rd ed. (Homewood, IL: Dorsey Press, 1984); and Peter Sheras and Steve Worchel, *Clinical Psychology: A Social-Psychological Approach* (New York: Van Nostrand, 1979).
13. Martin E. P. Seligman, *Helplessness* (San Francisco: W. H. Freeman, 1975).
14. See, for example, E. J. Phares, *Locus of Control in Personality* (Morristown, NJ: General Learning Press, 1976).
15. See, for example, J. Harvey, W. Ickes, and R. Kidd, eds., *New Directions in Attribution Research,* Vol. 2 (Hillsdale, NJ: Lawrence Erlbaum Associates, 1978; especially the article by Carol S. Dweck and Therese E. Goetz, "Attributions and Learned Helplessness," pp. 157–79.
16. For a discussion of concepts like these as they relate specifically to the black experience see Kenneth B. Clark, *Dark Ghetto* (New York: Harper & Row, 1965); Robert

Coles, *Children of Crisis* (New York: Dell, 1967); James A. Banks and Jean D. Grambs, eds., *Black Self-Concept* (New York- McGraw-Hill, 1972); Stanley S. Guterman, ed., *Black Psyche* (Berkeley, CA: Glendessary Press, 1972); and Reginald L. Jones, ed., *Black Psychology* (New York: Harper & Row, 1980).

17. Jonathan H. Turner and Charles E. Starnes, *Inequality: Privilege and Poverty in America* (Pacific Palisades, CA: Goodyear, 1976), pp. 66–67.

18. Josiah Wedgewood, *The Economics of Inheritance* (London: George Routledge and Sons, 1929); for an update of Wedgewood's findings see C. D. Harbury, "The Inheritance and the Distribution of Personal Wealth in Britain," *Economic Journal* 72 (December 1962): 845–68.

19. See, for example, *Forbes*, September 13, 1982, pp. 99–186; *Forbes*, Fall 1983, pp. 49–192; *Forbes 400*, October 1, 1984 (Special Issue); *Forbes 400*, October 28, 1985 (Special Issue).

20. John A. Brittain, *Inheritance and the Inequality of Material Wealth* (Washington, DC: The Brookings Institution, 1978), p. 49.

21. Brittain, *Inheritance and Inequality*, p. 74.

22. John A. Brittain, *The Inheritance of Economic Status* (Washington, DC: The Brookings Institution, 1977).

23. Brittain, *Inheritance of Economic Status*, p. 15.

24. Paul Taubman, "The Determinants of Earnings: Genetics, Family, and other Environments; A Study of White, Male Twins" *American Economic Review* 66 (December 1976): 858–70; and Paul Taubman; *Income Distribution and Redistribution* (Reading, MA: Addison-Wesley, 1978).

25. Taubman, "Determinants of Earnings," pp. 866–67. While one of Taubman's purposes was to isolate the genetic and environmental aspects of family contribution to income, he and many others recognize the difficulty in partialing out the contribution of each family-related factor. His findings did, however, lead him to argue that the contribution of genetics was more important than environment.

26. Taubman, "Determinants of Earnings," p. 868.

27. Brittain, *Inheritance of Economic Status*, pp. 15–16.

28. Greg J. Duncan with Richard D. Coe, Mary E. Corcoran, Martha S. Hill, Saul D. Hoffman, and James N. Morgan, *Years of Poverty, Years of Plenty* (Ann Arbor: Survey Research Center, Institute for Social Research, University of Michigan, 1984).

29. Greg J. Duncan and James N. Morgan, "An Overview of Family Economic Mobility," in Greg J. Duncan et al., *Years of Poverty, Years of Plenty*, p. 10. Reprinted with permission.

4

States' Rights and Wrongs

The evolution of federalism in the United States has shown a relatively steady increase in the authority and responsibility of the national government and a concomitant lessening of the autonomy and independence of state and local governments. This process of history has not meant that states are unimportant or insignificant actors in our federal system. State and local governments retain—in fact they have continued to increase—their control and authority over and responsibility for many aspects of their citizens' lives. It is true, however, that in many areas of political, legal, social and economic affairs the national government directs and circumscribes the activities of state and local governments and narrows the parameters of their autonomy.

In general, although there are some notable exceptions, conservatives have argued for greater state autonomy vis-à-vis the national government. President Reagan and his administration have strongly asserted this position. In his first State of the Union address delivered on January 26, 1982, President Reagan said, "This administration has faith in state and local governments and the Constitutional balance envisioned by the founding fathers . . . .Our citizens feel they've lost control of even the most basic decisions made about the essential services of government, such as schools, welfare, roads, and even garbage collection. And they're right. . . . Together, after fifty years of taking power away from the hands of the people in their states and local communities we have started returning power and resources to them."[1] He followed these statements with a proposal for a huge program swap between the levels of government, which would essentially turn back 44 national grant programs to the states.[2]

An important assumption underlying the Reagan administration rhetoric and policy initiatives is that state and local governments are more effective, efficient, and are greater repositories of democratic values and institutions than is the national government. This assumption has led conservatives to feel that states' prerogatives vis-à-vis the national government must be vigilantly safeguarded and promoted. The acceptance of this line of thought has led conservatives to argue, implicitly and explicitly, that states are uniquely qualified to make the major domestic political decisions affecting the U.S. citizenry.

Most U.S. citizens do not fully accept the Reagan position regarding the failure of the national government and the superiority of decentralized power and authority. It is true that over the past several years, citizen confidence in the national government has waned, but it does not necessarily follow that this diminution in support for the national government has been accompanied by significant increases in support for state and local governments.

One of the most comprehensive studies of citizen support of various levels of government was conducted in 1973 for the Subcommittee on Intergovernmental Relations of the Committee on Government Operations of the United States Senate.[3] As Table 4.1 indicates, this study reports a general lack of high confidence for most societal institutions, including all levels of government.

As shown in Table 4.2, when asked specifically about their level of confidence in national, state, and local governments compared with five years earlier, few citizens reported greater confidence in any level, while substantial proportions of the sample had less confidence in all three levels. It is true that while all three levels were viewed with less confidence in the 1973 study, the national government was the least favorably viewed. Although, however, 72 percent of those interviewed in the 1973 study agreed with the statement that local governments were closer to the people and should be given more responsibility, 67 percent also felt that it was time for a strong central government to get things moving again. These contradictory views led Laurence O'Toole to conclude that there was "some basic confusion in the public mind about where power should rest."[4] One can hardly call these complex feelings a ringing endorsement of state and local governmental power over national governmental power.

The position of the national government vis-à-vis state and local authorities also improved in the 1973 study when respondents were asked which level of government could better handle specific problems. Here, the superior position of the national government in the minds of citizens becomes clear. Tucker and Zeigler point out that "there is little doubt—even when there is sentiment for sharing functions—that the federal government is viewed as the more appropriate problem solver by the public. . . . of 26 possible functions, the federal government was assigned major responsibility in 14, state government 5, and local government 7. . . . It seems fairly clear that the problems which Americans regard as most urgent are viewed as the appropriate domain of the federal government."[5]

This issue of governmental trust is quite complicated. Perhaps it can be clarified by bringing in data from some other studies. In their 1968, 1972, 1974, and 1976 postelection surveys, researchers at the Center for Political Studies at the

Table 4.1

Levels of Confidence in People Running U.S. Institutions, 1973 (percent expressing various levels of confidence)

Institutions	High	Medium	Low
Major companies	29%	44%	20%
Organized religion	36	35	22
Higher education institutions	44	37	15
U. S. Senate	30	48	18
Organized labor	20	41	32
The press	30	45	21
U. S. House of Representatives	29	49	15
Medicine	57	31	19
Television news	41	43	14
Local tax assessment	19	40	30
U. S. Supreme Court	33	40	21
Local government	28	49	19
State highway systems	34	43	17
Local public schools	39	36	18
State government	24	55	17
Local police department	44	36	18
Executive branch of federal government	19	39	34
Local United Fund	35	35	20
Local trash collection	52	27	12
The military	40	35	19
The White House	18	36	41
Law firms	24	49	20

Source: U.S. Congress, Senate, Committee on Government Operations, Subcommittee on Intergovernmental Relations, Confidence and Concern: Citizens View American Government, reported in David B. Hill and Norm Luttbeg, Trends in American Electoral Behavior (Itasca, ILL: Peacock, 1980), p. 121.

Table 4.2

Confidence in National, State, and Local Governments (1973), Compared to Five Years Earlier (percent selecting each option)

Level of Government	More	Less	Same	Not Sure
National	11	57	28	4
State	14	26	53	7
Local	13	30	50	7

Source: Confidence and Concern: Citizens View American Government. Subcommittee on Intergovernmental Relations, Committee on Government Operations, United States Senate, 1973, pp. 42-43.

Table 4.3
Faith in Level of Government, 1968–1976 (percent of respondents)

	Year			
Level Most Trusted	1968	1972	1974	1976
National	51	46	32	32
State	20	24	30	28
Local	29	30	38	40

Source: American National Election Studies, Post-Election Surveys, Center for Political Studies, University of Michigan, Ann Arbor: InterUniversity Consortium for Political and Social Research, 1969, 1973, 1975, 1977.

University of Michigan questioned respondents about their degrees of faith in the three levels of government, asking them in which level of government they had the most faith. The results from all four surveys are summarized in Table 4.3. The findings present some support for the president's position. In 1976, compared to 1968, 19 percent fewer respondents said that they placed greatest faith in the national government. And from the period 1968 to 1976, both state and local governments grew in the proportion of citizens who placed their greatest faith in them, 8 and 11 percent growth, respectively. What is also clear from the data, however, is that compared to the other two levels, the national government is still viewed relatively favorably by U.S. citizens. More citizens in 1976 placed greater faith in the national government than in their state governments, and while more placed faith in their local governments than in either state or national, the gap between local and national was not huge.

The Michigan researchers last asked the faith questions in 1976. For the past several years, however, the Advisory Commission on Intergovernmental Relations has asked a similar question: "From which level of government do you feel you get the most for your money—federal, state, or local?" Responses to this question, from 1973 to 1986, are reported in Table 4.4. The results are consistent with the Michigan findings. While there have been minor ups and downs for all three levels over the years, the overall trend is relatively consistent. Americans place their greatest confidence in federal and local levels (about one-third supporting) and their least confidence in state governments (about one-fifth supporting).

Two other similar items asked by yet another pollster, Gallup, point out the complex view citizens have of their various levels of government and the relatively positive place of the federal government in these evaluations. From 1973 to 1985, Gallup asked national samples how much confidence they had in various U.S. institutions. Two of these institutions were Congress and public schools. In 1973 Americans placed somewhat more faith in public schools than in Con-

Table 4.4
Level of Government Providing Citizens with the Best Return on Their Money

Percent of U.S. Public

	May 1986	May 1985	May 1984	May 1983	May 1982	Sept. 1981	May 1980	May 1979	May 1978	May 1977	March 1976	May 1975	April 1974	May 1973
Federal	32	32	24	31	35	30	33	29	35	36	36	39	29	35
Local	33	31	35	31	28	33	26	33	26	26	25	25	28	25
State	22	22	27	20	20	25	22	22	20	20	20	20	24	18
Don't Know	13	15	14	19	17	14	19	16	19	18	19	17	19	22

Source: Advisory Commission on Intergovernmental Relations. Changing Public Attitudes on Governments and Taxes, 1986, p. 4.

gress (58 and 42 percent, respectively, placing a "great deal" or "quite a lot" of confidence in the two institutions). By 1985, however, the public schools, a local government activity, had dropped to only 48 percent confidence, a loss of 10 percent, while Congress had dropped to 39 percent, a loss of only 3 percent. Both institutions had dropped in confidence, but the drop was more precipitous for the local institutions than for the national.[6]

The second item Gallup dealt with was the honesty and ethical standards of various professions. He asked a sample of Americans in 1985 how they rated the honesty and ethical standards of people in different fields, including U.S. senators and congressmen and state and local political officeholders. The responses given in this 1985 survey hardly indicate a ground swell of support for local and state officials vis-à-vis national ones. Gallup found that 23 percent of the respondents rated senators very high or high in ethical standards and honesty, 20 percent so rated congressmen, while only 18 percent gave this mark to local officials and only 15 percent rated state officials at this level of honesty.[7] Again, the myth of greater trust and confidence in local and state officials vis-à-vis national ones is not supported by the empirical evidence.

Feelings about taxes further illustrate the complexity of U.S. citizens' evaluation of these three branches of government. While 36 percent of citizens interviewed in a 1982 national survey felt that the federal income tax was the worst tax, 30 percent of the respondents said local property taxes were the worst.[8] The idea that over the past 50 years U.S. citizens have lost confidence in their national government and transferred this confidence to their state and local governments is an oversimplification of a vastly complex issue.

It is clear, however, that the conservative position, while oversimplified and incomplete, is not completely without foundation. For this reason, and because of President Reagan's success and the increased legitimacy of the new conservative agenda in U.S. politics, conservatives have begun a renewed and more vehement call for greater governmental decentralization and a vesting of greater power and responsibility in state and local governments. Many people today may be swayed by such arguments because they are not very familiar with the nature of federalism in U.S. politics, nor are they very familiar with the forces that led the national government to assume greater responsibility for citizens' well-being. We may need, therefore, to be reminded of the operations of U.S. federalism and of the actual record of states and local governments in performing their basic duties toward their citizens.

The first observation any student of U.S. national politics will make concerning our particular brand of federalism is that it is, and has been, an important and vital element in our political system. The sharing of powers between states and the national government, which characterizes our federal system, has helped moderate our political conflicts and stabilize and direct our democratic processes.

States and local governments have been and continue to be important forces in U.S. politics. The approximately 80,000 state and local governments raise and spend huge sums of money, employ very large numbers of workers, and regulate, control, and direct significant aspects of our everyday lives. In 1982 there were 3.76 million state employees and 9.23 million local employees, up 123 and 78 percent, respectively, from their 1962 levels. During that same 20-year period, the level of federal employment increased only 12 percent, from 2.54 million to 2.85 million employees.[9]

And while it is true that federal government expenditures have increased in the past 25 years, the same is true for state and local expenditures. Taking intergovernmental transfers into account, in 1954 the federal government spent 5.5 percent of the GNP, while states spent 2.9 percent and local governments 5.3 percent. By 1981 the federal portion of GNP spent had risen to 14 percent, but the percent spent by states and local governments had also risen sharply, to 5.4 and 8.6 percent, respectively.[10] Not only are they spending more, state and local governments are incurring greater debt. Between 1961 and 1975 state and local debt increased 261 and 171 percent, respectively. The federal debt during that same period increased 86 percent.[11]

States and local governments are certainly very important in the scheme of U.S. politics, with the decentralization of power and authority they represent providing important benefits to our system. David Nice has summarized the benefits of decentralization found in U.S. federalism: greater flexibility, checks and balances, greater responsiveness and efficiency, conflict resolution, opportunities for increased participation, self-reliance, and innovation.[12]

This is only one side of the decentralization phenomenon, however. There is another, more negative reality concerning decentralization, which must also be acknowledged. The problems are many and include inequality, discrimination, limited actual participation, elite dominance, and serious program failures. These problems were a principal, motivating force behind the growth in responsibility and influence of the national government. Let us look at some of them in greater detail.

Because of their relative freedom and autonomy, states were free to engage in a great deal of discriminatory activity, and many did so with a vengeance. As Henry Steele Commager has pointed out, "it was the states that maintained slavery, the national government that abolished it. It was the states that fought for slavery and tried to reinstate it, through 'black codes,' even after Appomattox. It was the national government that intervened with the Thirteenth, Fourteenth, and Fifteenth amendments and a succession of civil rights acts designed to emancipate and free."[13]

The way in which the states, particularly the southern ones, restricted the freedoms of their black citizens is perhaps the blackest mark against U.S. federalism and the greatest example of the problems that can arise in a heavily decentralized intergovernmental system. Two of the most significant areas of state discrimination, education and voting, are discussed in detail below.

The barriers that southern state governments erected to disenfranchise their black citizens can best be described as thorough, inventive, prolific, and varied. Even before the formal end of the Reconstruction period, the actions of some

southern state governments and numerous white organizations had already succeeded in intimidating southern blacks and significantly limiting black political
participation.[14] The end of Reconstruction brought the "legal" disenfranchise-
ment of southern blacks by southern state governments. The litany of discriminatory devices is well known: literacy tests, white primaries, poll taxes, yearly
registration, and a myriad of administrative procedures that made it virtually
impossible for most blacks to register and participate in southern politics.[15] Bass
and DeVries have pointed out the particularly severe restrictions imposed on
blacks voting in many southern states at the turn of the century. In 1900 Alabama
had more than 78,000 registered black voters in just 14 "black belt" counties;
by 1903 this number had been reduced to only 1,081. In Louisiana in 1898 there
were over 130,000 registered black voters; in 1900 the number was reduced to
only 5,230.[16]

As late as 1960, the estimated percentage of voting-age blacks registered to
vote in the 11 southern states ranged from a low of only 6 percent in Mississippi
to 48 percent in Tennessee.[17] The limited voting-protection provisions of the
1957, 1960, and 1964 civil rights acts had helped somewhat, but by the end of
1964 there still existed a large body of unregistered black citizens.[18]

It took the strong intervention of the national government in the form of the
1965 Voting Rights Act to change substantially this situation. The rush of eligible
and interested black citizens registering after the implementation of the act was
remarkable. Table 4.5 shows the pre-and post–1965 Voting Rights Act registration figures for the 11 southern states. It is not difficult to see the marked
increase in black registration levels in the short interval after implementation of
the act. As Commager pointed out, to correct the wrong perpetrated against
black citizens by their southern state governments took a very long time and the
very serious intervention of the national government.

The record of southern states in the area of public education was equally
dismal. The systematic and purposeful neglect and deprivation that state educational systems visited upon their black children was nothing less than appalling.
In addition to segregation itself, the poorer facilities and institutions, lower
expenditures, and less-qualified instructors indicate the moral injustice that occurred under a relatively decentralized federalism system with strong state autonomy and limited central government oversight.

The following few examples illustrate the magnitude of the problem. In expenditures per pupil in the school year 1949–50, Georgia spent $79.73 per Negro
student and $145.15 per white student, while Mississippi spent $122.93 per
white student and only $32.55 per Negro child.[19] Per capita college expenditures
in 1950–51 show Arkansas spending $1,143.22 per white student and $536.28
per Negro student, while Louisiana was spending $1,333.62 per white student
and only $597.10 per Negro student.[20] In 1940, capital outlays per pupil in
Alabama amounted to $6.68 per white pupil and $0.62 per Negro pupil.[21] A
study conducted in 1940 showed that white school teachers in Georgia averaged
3.0 years of college, while Negroes averaged 1.7. Alabama was a little better,

Table 4.5
Pre- and Post-1965 Voting Rights Act Black Registration Levels for the 11 Southern States

State	Pre–Act Reg.[a] Percentage	Post–Act Reg.[b] Percentage
Alabama	19.3	51.6
Arkansas	40.4	62.8
Florida	51.2	63.6
Georgia	27.4	52.6
Louisiana	31.6	58.9
Mississippi	6.7	59.8
North Carolina	46.8	51.3
South Carolina	37.3	51.2
Tennessee	69.5	71.7
Texas	@	61.6
Virginia	38.3	55.6

@Separate black and white figure for Texas Pre-Act are not available.

[a]Pre-Act figures from March, 1965

[b]Post-Act figures from September, 1967

Source: United States Commission on Civil Rights, <u>Political Participation</u>, 1968, pp. 222–223.

with whites averaging 3.2 years and Negroes 2.1.[22] Yearly salaries of classroom teachers in 1940 tell a similar story. Alabama whites received $848, while Negroes received $487; Louisiana whites received $1,047 compared to $390 for Negroes; Mississippi paid its white teachers $776 and its Negro ones $232.[23] Library facilities were also unequal. In 1940 Louisiana had 3.2 books per white student and 0.5 per Negro; Georgia had 3.0 per white and 0.5 per Negro; and South Carolina had 2.3 per white and 0.7 per Negro student.[24]

Even more damning is the fact that almost all of this substantially inferior investment was occurring in an overwhelmingly segregated school environment. The 1967 *Report of the U.S. Commission on Civil Rights* documents the extent of this segregation in northern as well as southern schools. The report shows that in 20 selected large school districts across the country, ranging from Richmond, Virginia, to Chicago, Illinois, from Houston, Texas, to Miami, Florida, the number of black elementary school students attending 90–100 percent Negro schools seldom dropped below 90 percent for the 10 southern cities and was only slightly better for a few of the northern ones.[25]

Figures like these point out the incredible racially based inequality that can be, and was, imposed in a decentralized federal system with high state autonomy and limited national government oversight. Many of the racially based social, economic, and political problems we are dealing with today grew out of the inequalities imbedded in our society during this period of relatively unfettered state and local autonomy in the area of civil and political rights.

In addition to the targeted, within-state, racially motivated inequality noted above, important other inequalities can arise in the decentralized federalism endorsed so strongly by the conservatives. These are differences, across and within states, in level of services and levels of taxation that place significantly different burdens on different groups of citizens. And these differences can, in some cases, be profound, significantly affecting the quality of life, or even life itself, for many citizens.

The first thing one observes when examining the taxing and expenditure patterns in the states is their extreme variation. In the area of education, for example, some states spend substantially larger sums of money on their children's educations than do others. In 1980, excluding Alaska, per capita state and local expenditures on education ranged from a high of $914 in Wyoming to $475 in Arkansas.[26] And states differ significantly in the extent to which they provide assistance to local school districts. In 1978 the state percentage of local school costs ranged from a low of 6.3 percent in New Hampshire to a high of 82.8 percent in Hawaii.[27] While differing costs of living across states will account for some of the difference in per capita expenditures, it is clear that some states are, at the margins, investing substantially greater resources in the education of their children than are others.

Not only do state educational efforts differ from one another; state policies result in quite different levels of educational effort across school districts in the same state. States like Texas, which depend heavily on local property taxes to support schools, place significantly different burdens on poor and rich school districts and provide highly variable programs, depending on the wealth of the local district. The result is that wealthy districts with a high level of assessed property valuation, like Highland Park, can provide many more dollars per student at a much lower rate of taxation. The result is a system in which lower-wealth districts, like San Antonio, tax themselves at equal or even higher rates, but are still able to provide only a fraction of the expenditure per pupil of the wealthier districts.

States also differ substantially in the degree to which they provide support and services to their citizens in need. First, many states have been reluctant even to participate in federal programs that provide benefits to the poor. In 1965, at the beginning of the Food Stamp program, only 29 states were participating. It was not until 1974 that all 50 states enrolled in the program.[28] And while they may participate in the Food Stamp, Medicaid, or AFDC programs, states differ substantially in their levels of contributions to these programs. The result is a wide range in benefit levels across states for the same federally sponsored program. For example, yearly AFDC benefits for a family of four ranged in 1979 from a high of $6,552 in Hawaii to a low of $1,440 in Mississippi.[29] The percentage of state and local contributions to welfare programs in 1977–78 ranged from a high of 74.2 percent in Alaska to a low of 27.5 percent in Alabama.[30]

Some states are, without question, providing greater services to their needy populations than are others.

Not only do states differ significantly from one another on the expenditure side, they differ substantially on the level of their tax effort and distribution of their tax burden. Assigning the U.S. average state tax effort a score of 100, in 1983 states ranged from a tax effort of 163 in New York to 64 in Nevada.[31] States also place different tax burdens on different categories of their citizens. State taxes in general are quite regressive, placing heavier burdens, per unit of income, on their poorer citizens, but many states do a better job of balancing the tax burden across categories of citizen income. Minnesota and California are two of the most balanced states on tax burden. In 1974 a family with an income of $5,000 in Minnesota paid 12.7 percent of its income in state and local taxes, while a family making $50,000 paid 11.8 percent of its income in state and local taxes. The figures for California were 11.8 and 10.8 percent respectively. Among the many states placing a much greater relative tax burden on their poorer than on their wealthier citizens were New Hampshire (12.3 percent and 5.1 percent) and Texas (9.3 percent and 3.5 percent).[32]

There are many who might argue that the wide-ranging differences in expenditure and service level across states is exactly what one hopes to achieve in a decentralized system. Those states whose citizens want to provide less or spend less on certain categories have the right to do so. Those who argue that these disparities mark real and purposive choices by citizens of states must, however, face certain unpleasant realities. The first is that these disparities are often due less to a state's will than to its fiscal ability. The levels of wealth across states and localities are quite varied, and more often than not, lower expenditure levels are the result of lower levels of income and economic development across jurisdictions.[33] Those who spend less usually do so because their economic circumstances provide them with less to spend.

The second reality relates to politics and control. There are certainly those jurisdictions that spend less, even though relative wealth levels may be high and relative tax effort may be low. Here, historical trends, long legal precedents in the form of statutes or constitutional amendments, which require large majorities to overturn, and established power structures and ruling oligarchies make higher levels of expenditures difficult to implement, even though large numbers of citizens may actually support them.

This, then, brings us to one of the most crucial assumptions underlying the conservative position supporting strong grants of power and authority to state and local governments: that they are "closer to the people," and are truly grassroots, democratic units, which, unlike the national government, really represent the will of the citizens. Is this an accurate reflection of democratic processes at the state and local level? In general, it is not.

The fact is that state and local governments have historically not done very well on the democracy dimension. Problems that have made the rhetoric of closer-to-the-people ring somewhat hollow include malapportionment, low levels of participation and information, discriminatory structures, and lack of significant political and party competition.

A major problem that for many years seriously restricted democratic participation in state and local affairs was malapportionment. As the nation shifted its population base from a rural to an urban population, political jurisdictions did not follow. Geographical areas used to demarcate political jurisdictions were left unchanged, even though many were emptied and others became overstocked. The result was a system of state legislative districts appallingly out of balance. As late as 1964, states as diverse as Louisiana and Maine had legislative districts ranging in population size from 6,000 to 58,000 in Louisiana and 3,900 to 10,500 in Maine. The situation was similar throughout most of the 50 states.[34] While a similar problem existed for congressional districts, one must remember that it was the responsibility of state legislatures to draw these district boundaries, and it was state governments' failure to execute their responsibilities that underenfranchised millions of state citizens and overenfranchised millions of others.

In addition to the general undemocratic nature of such malapportionment, state electoral structures further restricted full democratic participation by many of their citizens. We have already mentioned individual voter discrimination devices used by states to restrict black voting, but there are a number of other structural arrangements that have made it difficult for many state citizens to participate fully in the governance of their state and localities. Nonpartisan elections and at-large and multimember electoral districts have reduced turnout levels, raised the costs of campaigns, and held down the number of minority officeholders.[35] These structures have helped keep the number of minority and female officeholders very low[36] and have helped white, middle- and upper-class professional males to dominate state legislative bodies.[37]

We tend to think of state and local governments as the last bastion of "direct" democracy in the United States, and it is true that it is at this level that we see the initiative, referendum, and recall practices at work. States differ substantially, however, in the degree to which they allow these direct democratic processes. Of the 50 states, only 17 allow a constitutional initiative, 21 allow state statutory initiatives, 32 local statutory initiatives, 38 local statutory referenda, and 39 state statutory referenda.[38]

One of the cornerstones of democratic government is citizen participation in elections. Conservative rhetoric concerning the greater democratic opportunities in state and local settings implies that, because they are closer to the people there surely must be high levels of citizen participation in and knowledge of state and local political affairs. This expectation is not correct, however. Turnout of registered or eligible voters in state and local political contests falls far short of the levels in national elections. Median voter turnout in all city elections, including those held in conjunction with state and national races, was only 29 percent in 1975; and as the previous structural argument suggested, the turnout levels in reformed cities, those with nonpartisan elections, was below that in partisan cities, 36 and 27 percent, respectively.[39] And it is not unusual for local municipal, school board, or bond elections to have less than 15 percent voter participation.

This low participation rate is related to a substantial lack of knowledge about and interest in state and local affairs. In two studies conducted by this author, few citizens surveyed in two Texas cities could name their mayor or any of their city councilmen.[40] And in a nationwide study of mayors and councilmen reported in 1974, city officials reported that most of the things their citizens complained about related to issues like animal control and traffic.[41] These are not issues at the cutting edge of democratic debate.

Not only does the state and local record on democratic governance leave much to be desired, but state and local program effectiveness does not give much of a boost to state and local images, either. If conservatives feel that turning programs over to state and local governments will result in better-managed programs, it would be interesting to ask them which exemplary programs they can point to in order to illustrate their position. Three of the most important responsibilities left almost completely in the hands of state and local officials, with very little federal interference or guidance, are education (excluding the issue of segregation), non-aged health care, and transportation. While many states are trying very hard in these areas, the general record of states and local governments in running these programs is poorer than even many states, themselves, would like.

President Reagan's own National Commission on Excellence in Education, in their report entitled *A Nation at Risk: The Imperative for Educational Reform*, chronicles the substantial shortcomings of state and local school systems in failing to provide an adequate educational system for citizens of this country.[42] A separate report, *Hard Choices*, prepared for the Joint Economic Committee of Congress, chronicles state, local, and federal failures in maintaining the educational, transportation, and physical infrastructure of our nation.[43] A substantial portion of this failure can be laid directly at the doorstep of state and local governments.

In the area of health, the state and local record is equally troubling. *Hunger in America*, a study completed by the Harvard University School of Public Health in 1985, examines the failure of many state and local governments to provide adequate health and nutritional care for their poor citizens and notes the increasing rate of infectious disease and infant mortality as a result of this neglect.[44] And just looking at the managerial dimension, the charity health program run primarily by state and local governments—Medicaid—fares poorly on most comparisons with the federally controlled program, Medicare. On every dimension, from fraud to numbers of doctors participating to reimbursement schedules, the performance of the state-based Medicaid program comes in a poor second to the federally managed Medicare program.[45]

With reports like these, one might wonder how anyone would continue to seek to transfer new, unsupervised responsibilities to the state and local governments, but this would be too harsh a reaction. States and local governments do many things well, and citizens have developed, over the years, positive feelings toward these entities. It is true, however, that one's ideological predispositions do seem to color these feelings.

Table 4.6 reports faith in levels of government, by political ideology, for a national sample of U.S. citizens interviewed in 1976. Conservatives definitely place less faith in the national government and more faith in local governments than do liberals, but they place less faith in state governments than in the national government. Liberals place similar levels of faith in the federal and local governments and the least faith, like conservatives, in state governments. Whether these positions arise out of attachments to normative democratic theories or personal or group self-interest, these data cannot tell us.

Many cynics would argue that at least some of the impetus behind the conservative push for decentralization is grounded not in ideological purity but in personal self-interest. Is it really that conservatives feel the demands of democracy require greater state and local power, or are they simply seeking the advantages this decentralization offers? Do conservative fundamentalist Protestants really prefer state regulation over federal regulation in general, or do they simply find that the federal level has denied them what they may still be able to get from states? It was, after all, a state law concerning school textbooks that brought religious fundamentalists into federal court for relief. And it is state and local laws regarding zoning that have brought realtors and businessmen into federal court to seek greater "freedom" regarding the use of their property. And it was a state law requiring mental-health coverage that was challenged by insurance companies in Massachusetts as exceeding federal requirements.

Many who oppose federal regulation and control may support states' rights arguments, not out of an ideological commitment to state sovereignty as a fundamental principal of democracy, but as a mechanism to avoid regulation they feel less likely at the state level.

CONCLUSION

This chapter has examined the record of U.S. state and local governments on civil rights, democratic governance, and equal opportunities and burdens for their citizens. The analysis has demonstrated a quite different picture of state and local citizen relations than that implied by conservatives. It has shown that states and local governments have historically been more discriminatory than has been the national government. In addition, data presented on state and local government structures, and on the low levels of citizen knowledge of, and participation in, state and local affairs, raise important questions about the supposed greater "democratic" content conservatives assign to these levels of government.

States have an important role to play in regulating citizen affairs and delivering services. Removing national government oversight from many areas of governmental action may, however, have significantly negative impacts on large groups

Table 4.6
Faith in Level of Government, by Political Ideology, 1976 (percent of respondents)

Level Most Trusted	Ideology		
	Liberal	Moderate	Conservative
National	35	37	26
State	28	27	29
Local	37	36	46

Source: American National Election Study, Post-election study, Center for Political Studies, University of Michigan, Ann Arbor: Inter-university Consortium for Political and Social Research, 1977.

of citizens and may serve only to weaken service delivery standards and to highten political, economic, legal, and social inequality in the U.S. society.

The principal question we as citizens must ask is, What is an appropriate division of authority and responsibility between the levels of government that is commensurate with a level of services and rights required by national citizenship? We have seen that an ideologically based assertion of the greater effectiveness, efficiency, or democraticness of state and local governments is not supported by the empirical evidence. These findings do not mean that state and local governments are unimportant or insignificant, or that they should be denied important powers. It means that sorting out the important responsibilities for our citizens and assigning them to various levels of government should be based on the true abilities of that level to fairly and effectively execute those responsibilities. We cannot and should not blindly assign responsibility out of unsupportable ideological assumptions about who can and should perform a particular set of functions.

NOTES

1. President Ronald Reagan, State of the Union Message, reported in *New York Times*, January 27, 1982, p. 16.

2. For a discussion of the Reagan federalism initiative, see J. L. Sedgwick, "The Prospects of 'Restoring the Federal Balance'," *Polity* 17, (Fall 1984): 66–87.

3. U.S. Congress, Senate, Committee on Government Operations, Subcommittee on Intergovernmental Relations, *Confidence and Concern: Citizens View American Government*. December 3, 1973.

4. Laurence J. O'Toole, Jr. *American Intergovernmental Relations* (Washington DC: Congressional Quarterly Press, 1985), p. 80.

5. L. H. Zeigler and H. J. Tucker, *The Quest for Responsive Government: An Introduction to State and Local Politics* (North Scituate, MA: Duxbury Press, 1978), p. 26.

6. *Gallup* Report, #238, July 1985, p. 3.

7. *Gallup Report,* #238, August 1985, p. 3.

8. Advisory Commission on Intergovernmental Relations, *Changing Public Attitudes on Government and Taxes: A Commission Survey* (Washington, DC: ACIR, 1982), p. 4.

9. Michael Dowling, "Innovation in State Policymaking: A Review of the Literature," Houston Area Research Center, The Woodlands Center for Growth Studies, May 1986.

10. Roy Bahl, *Financing State and Local Government in the 1980s* (New York: Oxford University Press, 1984), pp. 10–11.

11. Nicholas Henry, *Governing at the Grassroots: State and Local Politics* (Englewood Cliffs, NJ: Prentice-Hall, 1980), pp. 320–21.

12. David C. Nice, *Federalism: The Politics of Intergovernmental Relations* (New York: St. Martin's Press, 1987), pp. 13–16.

13. Henry Steele Commager, "Tocqueville's Mistake: A Defense of Strong Central Government," *Harper's* 269:1611 (August 1984): 70–74.

14. Kenneth M. Stampp, *The Era of Reconstruction 1865–1877* (New York: Vintage Books, 1965), pp. 74–82.

15. For an elaboration of the extensive voting barriers erected by southern governments see T. I. Emerson, D. Haber, and N. Dorsen, *Political and Civil Rights in the United States,* students' ed. Vol. 2 (Boston: Little, Brown, 1967); and V. O. Key, *Southern Politics* (New York: Vintage Books, 1949), pp. 533–643.

16. Charles Press and Kenneth VerBurg, *State and Community Governments in the Federal System* (New York: Wiley, 1979), p. 4321.

17. Donald R. Matthews and James W. Prothro, *Negroes and the New Southern Politics* (New York: Harcourt, Brace and World, 1966), p. 148.

18. Matthews and Prothro, *Negroes,* pp. 18–19.

19. Joint Commission of the National Education Association and the American Teachers Association, *Study of the Status of the Education of Negroes, Part 2,* January 1954, p. 25.

20. Joint Commission, *Education of Negroes,* p. 41.

21. Harry S. Ashmore, *The Negro and the Schools.* (Chapel Hill: University of North Carolina Press, 1954), p. 156.

22. Ashmore, *The Negro and Schools,* p. 158.

23. Ashmore, *The Negro and Schools,* p. 159.

24. Ashmore, *The Negro and Schools,* p. 160.

25. U.S. Commission on Civil Rights, *Racial Isolation in the Public Schools* (Washington, DC: U.S. Government Printing Office, 1967), p. 7.

26. John A. Straayer. *American State and Local Government,* 3rd ed. (Columbus, OH: Charles E. Merrill, 1983), p. 409.

27. Frederick M. Wirt, "Institutionalization: Prison and School Policies," in *Politics in the American State* ed. Virginia Gray, Herbert Jacob, and Kenneth N. Vines, (Boston: Little, Brown 1983), 4th ed., pp. 287–328.

28. Advisory Commission on Intergovernmental Relations, *Public Assistance: The Growth of a Federal Function* (Washington, DC: ACIR, July 1980), p. 82.

29. Advisory Commission, *Public Assistance,* p. 112.

30. Robert B. Albritton, "Subsidies: Welfare and Transportation," in Gray et al., *Politics,* pp. 312–13.

31. Advisory Commission on Intergovernmental Relations, *Significant Features of Fiscal Federalism 1985–86* (Washington, DC: February 1986), pp. 85–86, 131.

32. Nicholas Henry, *Governing at the Grassroots,* pp. 312–13.

33. For a discussion of the relationship between state economic development levels and public policy expenditures see Thomas R. Dye, *Politics, Economics and the Public* (Chicago: Rand McNally, 1966).

34. Leroy Hardy, Alan Heslop, and Stuart Anderson, eds, *Reapportionment Politics: The History of Redistricting in the 50 States.* Beverly Hills, CA: Sage Publications, 1981).

35. For a discussion of some of these issues in local elections see Albert K. Karnig and Susan Welch, "Electoral Structure and Black Representation on City Councils," *Social Science Quarterly (March 1982). 99–114,* Arnold Vedlitz and Charles Johnson, "Community Segregation, Electoral Structure and Minority Representation," *Social Science Quarterly* 63 (December 1982): 729–36.

36. *1985 Municipal Yearbook* (Washington, DC: International City Management Association, 1985), pp. 258–59.

37. Michael Engel, *State and Local Politics* (New York: St. Martin's Press, 1985), pp. 107–11.

38. Advisory Commission on Intergovernmental Relations, *Citizen Participation in the American Federal System* (Washington, DC: ACIR, 1977), p. 248.

39. Albert K. Karnig and V. O. Walters, "Municipal Elections: Registration, Incumbent Success, and Voter Participation," in *1977 Municipal Year Book* (Washington, DC: International City Management Association, 1977), p. 70.

40. Arnold Vedlitz, *Public Information, Citizen Feedback and Governmental Support in Garland, Texas*. Contract Report, U.S. Department of Housing and Urban Development and the League of Cities—Conference of Mayors, Inc., November, 1975; and C. Lamb, W. Pride, and A. Vedlitz, *Public Information and Citizen Feedback in Temple, Texas*. Contract Report for the U.S. Department of Housing and Urban Development, 1975.

41. David R. Berman, *State and Local Politics,* 2d. ed. (Boston: Allyn and Bacon, 1978), p. 231.

42. National Commission on Excellence in Education, *A Nation at Risk: The Imperative for Educational Reform* (Washington, DC: U.S. Education Department, 1983).

43. Deborah Matz', ed., "Hard Choices." A Study prepared for the use of the Subcommittee on Economic Goals and Intergovernmental Policy, Joint Economic Committee, United States Congress, February, 1984.

44. Physician Task Force on Hunger in America, *Hunger in America: The Growing Epidemic* (Boston: Harvard University School of Public Health, 1985).

45. For a thorough comparison of the Medicaid and Medicare programs, see "Twenty Years of Medicare and Medicaid," *Health Care Financing Review, 1985 Annual Supplement,* Washington, DC, Health Care Financing Administration, 1985.

5

Markets and Magic

In spite of recent problems—the increasing deficits, the balance-of-trade problems, the loss of industrial jobs, and so on—the fact remains that for over a century the United States has been an economic success story. Our levels of employment, our wage rates, our GNP growth, our productivity, and our standard of living are the envy of most of the world and have been for almost one hundred years. The United States has achieved this success through what economists call a mixed economy, a combination of government regulation and competitive markets.

This mixture of governmental interference and competitive market forces has engendered significant debate and controversy, however, over just what should be the proper roles of government and the private sector in any particular economic endeavor. There exists a theoretical continuum, ranging from completely free and unregulated markets on one end to totally regulated and controlled markets on the other.

Oftentimes discussions examining the relative merits of free and regulated markets degenerate into comparisons of socialistic or capitalistic economic systems, and it needs to be made clear that that is not the focus here. The important question is, rather, to recognize that capitalism itself is a very complex notion, with tremendous variations. Capitalist economies can exist within a relatively unregulated or relatively regulated context. When, therefore, one questions the merits of a particular version or concept of the free market, one is not necessarily arguing for a different, noncapitalist alternative. Rather, one may be simply selecting among a range of capitalistic alternatives, one either more or less subject to regulatory involvement than another.

These are the real choices faced by the U.S. citizenry. We have a capitalistic economy, which can be subject to varying degrees of regulation. Conservatives and liberals differ on the degree of regulation they seek for market-based exchanges. There is, however, relative consensus on a capitalistic solution; the disagreement occurs only on the relative degree of regulation and oversight of market exchanges sought by various ideological groupings.

Conservative U.S. spokesmen have argued forcefully for relatively unregulated markets. They support the ideal of free markets and believe that, in general, if left alone, market forces will produce better economic outcomes and better societal consequences than will governmentally regulated markets.[1] Much of their faith in the unregulated market stems from their acceptance of the basic economic principles laid down in the mid-eighteenth century by Adam Smith in his classic work the *Wealth of Nations*. Smith's position, put very simply, is that the greatest economic and social good will come through the unfettered competition of individuals pursuing their own self-interest. One of Smith's most important and most articulate modern-day disciples, Milton Friedman, summarized Smith's contribution this way:

> The key insight of Adam Smith's *Wealth of Nations* is misleadingly simple: if an exchange between two parties is voluntary, it will not take place unless both believe they will benefit from it. . . . Adam Smith's flash of genius was his recognition that the prices that emerged from voluntary transactions between buyers and sellers—for short, in a free market—could coordinate the activity of millions of people, each seeking his own interest, in such a way as to make everyone better off.[2]

This basic assertion, begun in Smith's eighteenth-century economic world and resurrected and applied to twentieth-century America by neoclassical economists such as Friedman, is the principal theoretical argument underlying current conservative policy positions opposing an active role for government in regulating the U.S. economy. It is a position strongly embraced by President Reagan and one that has guided much of his administration's approach to economic and social policy since he took office in 1981. President Reagan's strong belief in the importance and centrality of Smith's concept of the free market was illustrated in his enunciation of his "Economic Bill of Rights" on July 3, 1987. In this highly symbolic speech given at the Jefferson Memorial during the July 4th holiday celebration period, one of the four basic economic rights Mr. Reagan highlighted was the right to participate in a free market.[3]

While President Reagan and other conservatives made the free-market notion a centerpiece of their economic and social programs, it is not a position that is uniformly and consistently endorsed by the American people. In the abstract, of course, most Americans will support the notion of the free market. When asked, however, to evaluate specific applications and situations in which the concept of the free market and governmental regulation to promote certain activities come into conflict, the citizenry consistently seem very supportive of government regulation and intervention.

Each year, the Roper Center for Public Opinion Research conducts a General Social Survey of a representative sample of the U.S. public. In the most recent survey available for analysis, taken in 1985, respondents were asked to say whether or not they favored certain activities that the government might undertake for the economy. In what can be taken as a strong endorsement of the conservative position, an overwhelming majority of respondents were opposed to government control of prices and wages and supported less government regulation of business.[4] When one moves from these general control issues to specific assistance programs, however, one finds substantial citizen support for active government participation in the economy. Table 5.1 summarizes some of those citizen attitudes.

In this 1985 survey a substantial majority of Americans endorsed government support for industry to develop new products and technology and approved government financing of projects to create new jobs. A tiny minority, only 21 percent were opposed to government support of declining industries to protect jobs.

When examining specific areas of government spending, substantial pluralities, or majorities, of Americans wanted the government to spend more on the environment, health, police and law enforcement, retirement benefits, education, and unemployment benefits. Table 5.2 reports the survey findings.

While respondents did not want government to own any business enterprises, substantial pluralities wanted government to control prices and profits in the electric power industry, in local mass transportation, and in banking and insurance.[5] Even though, on an earlier question, respondents reported that they opposed government control of prices and wages, on later questions an overwhelming majority of respondents did feel it was the government's responsibility to keep prices under control, to provide health care for the sick, and to provide a decent standard of living for the old.[6] And large pluralities supported government's responsibility to provide industry with the help it needs to grow, and to provide a decent standard of living for the unemployed.[7]

These public sentiments and desires are hardly a ringing endorsement for trust in the free market to provide for their or for society's needs. Quite the contrary, it is a strong endorsement for active government participation in the economic concerns of the nation to ensure greater benefits for the nation's citizens. There are good reasons for the public not to be very supportive of the free-market doctrine and to prefer government intervention to make things better. Either through their direct experience or through their common sense, people recognize the weaknesses and limitations in the free-market doctrine and its lack of appropriateness for many aspects of U.S. economic and social life.

There are many reasons why the significant and powerful market mechanism described by Adam Smith cannot, and should not, be applied blindly to all aspects of modern economic life in the United States. In contrast to the relatively small, relatively competitive, and relatively accessible economic environment Smith encountered in essentially preindustrial England, "today's market mech-

Table 5.1
Citizen Attitudes toward Government Involvement in Economic Affairs, 1985
(percent of respondents)

Policy Area

% Respondents	Gov't Funding Projects to Create New Jobs	Gov't Support for Industry to Develop New Products + Tech.	Gov't Support for Declining Ind. to Protect Jobs
Supporting	68%	71%	51%
Neutral	16	18	22
Opposing	15	9	26
DK/NA	1	2	1

Source: James H. Davis and T. W. Smith, *General Social Surveys, 1972–1986* (Chicago: National Opinion Research Center, 1986), pp. 358–359.

Table 5.2
Citizen Attitudes toward Government Spending on Specific Policy Areas, 1985
(percent of respondents)

Policy Area

% Respondents Wanting to:	Environment	Health	Police and Law Enforc.	Education	Defense	Ret. Ben.	Unem. Ben.
Spend More	41%	56%	50%	62%	19%	41%	25%
Spend Same as Now	41	33	41	30	35	40	47
Spend Less	12	8	5	4	41	13	23
DK/NA	6	3	4	4	6	6	5

Source: James A. Davis and T. W. Smith, *General Social Surveys, 1972–1986* (Chicago: National Opinion Research Center, 1986), pp. 360–361.

anism is characterized by the huge size of its participants. . . . and the . . . infinitely more complex present-day production methods.''[8] Even strong neoclassical conservatives like Irving Kristol must admit that ''the capitalist economy and capitalist society have, in the course of their growth, been transformed into something very different from what Adam Smith had in mind. . . . there is little doubt that the ideal of a 'free market' in the era of large corporations, is not quite the original capitalist idea.''[9]

Hundreds of years have passed since Smith first articulated his economic theories, and many aspects of society have changed since his time. Conservatives have observed these changes and have adjusted to some aspects of the greater governmental role in the economy such changes have required. The fact remains, however, that the assertions and assumptions of modern conservatives, especially those associated with the Reagan administration, about the power of unregulated markets and the need to limit government economic activity, are grounded firmly in the principles laid down by Smith 300 years ago. Therefore, to understand and properly evaluate the economic policy positions of conservatives today, particularly their strong opposition to government economic activity, we must look closely at Smith's scheme and evaluate its appropriateness for our modern society.

In order to begin our evaluation of the appropriateness of Smith's free-market prescription for modern America, we must first articulate those conditions that Smith himself assumed or asserted must exist in order for the market mechanism to function properly. These conditions include competition, information, low market-entry costs, clear-cut and simple supply-and-demand-based provider/consumer exchanges, and a properly working contract-enforcement mechanism. In the relatively simple economic environment of the 1750s, many of these ideals could at least be approximated, if not actually met. The same cannot be said for the much more complex environment of twentieth-century America. Let us look in more detail at why these conditions, at least partially present in Adam Smith's day, cannot today serve as the justification for unregulated market competition as the principal allocator of goods and services in modern society.

COMPETITION AND MARKET ACCESS

In Adam Smith's world, firms were small and one could readily accept the assertion that many suppliers would either already exist in a market or that new entries could, with limited effort, convert existing enterprises or start new ones to capture a portion of attractive markets. Firms were small, and start-up and convertibility were seen as relatively low in cost. The expected result of all this available competition would be, of course, that the consumer would have maximum choice, thereby holding prices down and quality high.

The problem is that present-day enterprises are generally not the simple ones known to Smith. Most of our significant enterprises are huge corporations with large staffs, huge capital investments, huge distribution commitments, and huge debt structures. They are not the small, comfortable, flexible, and responsive enterprises envisioned by Smith. They are huge bureaucracies run, not by owners, but by professional management staffs. The extent of this largeness and con- centration in the present-day U.S. economic system is demonstrated in the degree of economic activity controlled by a very few large enterprises. Taking 1985 as our time point, there were over three million corporations doing business in the United States. The 500 largest corporations, making up only 0.01 percent of the total number of enterprises, in 1985 employed 13 percent of the total U.S. work force and possessed 28 percent of total U.S. corporate assets.[10]

These huge enterprises can insulate themselves from many of the short-term market forces Smith counted on to keep policies in line. They, often in con- junction with a few of their competitors, control large segments of important markets. And, because start-up costs for new competitors is prohibitively large in most cases, they can often ignore competition, especially domestic compe- tition, for substantially long periods of time. The result of all this lack of com- petition is that the consumer has very little to choose from, and this important aspect of Smith's self-correcting market mechanism cannot work. This problem is exacerbated in periods in which foreign competition is undeveloped or under- developed and U.S. firms with huge domestic market shares are essentially free to react not to external fears of competition, but to internal demands and goals. Such behavior may eventually catch up to these firms, as it has to steel and automobile manufacturers, but the length of time during which they could and did operate in virtually noncompetitive environments, and the damage that such non-self-regulating markets wreaked on our economic life when foreign com- petition did emerge, shows that there is no invisible hand efficiently and subtly guiding today's complex economic enterprises to the greatest social and economic good.

Information

Information about costs, product quality and product availability were as- sumed, by Smith, to be essential to a smooth working of his self-regulating market system. And, in that less complex time, appropriate information, while obviously not available to all buyers and sellers, was probably available to enough to serve a useful market-control purpose. One cannot say the same about the level of information needed by and possessed by buyers and sellers in today's complex marketplace. What are consumers buying today and what information is needed and available to buyers and sellers to help them make the rational and appropriate choices that are necessary to properly drive the self-correcting mar- ket?

The fact is that many products and services purchased by consumers today are quite technical or complex in nature. What makes a better vacuum cleaner or microwave oven? Which video cassette recorder or computer fuel-injection system will perform best for the price for the greatest length of time? Which lawyer or physician or insurance company truly provides the most appropriate and best service for the best price? How much disposable income will consumers have, and what types of goods and services are they likely to be wanting? Consumers, especially, have very little information on which to base these often expensive, or even life-saving, decisions. Manufacturers and service providers furnish little in the way of useful information, and what little there is is usually required by government regulators, not provided voluntarily as a service to information-conscious consumers. And what about consumers themselves? Are they the cautious, concerned, wary shoppers Smith needs them to be to act as the watchdogs of the self-correcting market?

In reality, they seem much more motivated by status needs, emotional attachments, or inertia than Smith would have them be. This is reflected in the mass advertising that product producers and service providers aim at American consumers. Romanticism, status, celebrity endorsements, and image, not information about product quality, cost, and competitive comparisons of important product qualities, are what a great deal of mass advertising provides the consuming public.

Sellers, too, often lack adequate information about what consumers want, how much they will buy, and what they are willing to pay. Again, the larger firms with high-powered marketing research staffs and advertising budgets have the edge over smaller firms in gauging trends in the marketplace and packaging products and services effectively to take advantage of consumer positions.

If advertising cannot or will not provide consumers the information they need (but may not want), and if only some firms can obtain much useful information on consumer trends, where can buyers and sellers look to help them make the rational choices needed to properly correct and direct the market? Perhaps the news media can look through the hype and image and confusion and provide interested buyers and sellers a more accurate picture of products and services. Alas, it would not appear that this is occurring. With the exception of a few business and consumer reporters in major markets, news organizations have not filled this void. They and their news organizations have neither the time, resources, nor expertise to evaluate fully product or service claims or gauge market trends. The plain fact is that in today's marketplace in the United States, appropriate information, that commodity viewed as so important in Smith's scheme, is often a rare commodity for many buyers and sellers.

Simple Provider–Consumer Exchanges

In Smith's scheme a buyer and a seller meet in the marketplace and work out the best deal between them. With both freely pursuing their self-interest, and because each has competing buyers and sellers, appropriate prices and product qualities are maintained—the market is regulated properly. The problem for modern society is that many, if not most, exchanges are not so straightforward. There are three basic differences between our market exchanges and those ideal ones described by Smith. One is that individuals, or individual-like small enterprises, are not usually found on both sides of today's exchanges. Certainly sellers, but in many cases buyers as well, are neither individuals nor representatives of small enterprises. Rather, they are agents of large, bureaucratic organizations, who may not be acting freely, may not be seeking their own interest, and may not have alternative buying and selling options.

A second difference is the fact that, in Smith's ideal, consumers are driven by their own desires and will to buy something they need. The initiation for the transaction is, therefore, consumer driven. This, too, is sometimes not the case in modern society. A person may suspect something is wrong with his health but the doctor, not the patient, largely decides what medical procedures and medicines are required, how long one will need to stay under care, and how frequently visits to the physician will be required. While a consumer may know that something is wrong with his Mercedes automobile, it will be the dealership (usually only one in most communities) that will tell him what is wrong, what must be done, and how much he must pay. Second opinions are possible in both the medical and automobile examples, but time, cost, and unavailability of viable and trusted competitors significantly reduce both consumers' options. In such exchanges, the seller directs both sides of the exchange. Self-correction is highly improbable in such cases.

The third factor that severely upsets the balance Smith seeks through simple, straightforward, buyer–seller exchanges is the critical problem of externalities. For Smith's exchange mechanism to work, the effects of transactions are assumed to be limited to the two affected parties—the buyer and seller. It is they, Smith tells us, whose selfish interests will guarantee to society the market regulation and best result. Exchanges in the complex modern world, and probably in Smith's simpler one as well, do not usually work this way. The impact of specific buyer–seller exchanges often extends far beyond those who directly participated in the exchange. Unique exchanges that may have been mutually beneficial and mutually agreeable to a specific buyer and seller may have significant, and often economically painful, repercussions to individuals and groups not direct parties to the exchange. These broader-reaching impacts are called externalities, and they may impose significant costs and penalties on economic participants who had absolutely nothing to do with the specific exchange.

Consider the following real-world example. Farmer Jones decides to dam a stream that runs through his property in order to irrigate his fields and provide power to turn a grist mill. He contracts with a dam builder to perform this work. They reach an amicable agreement between them as to the nature of the dam the contractor will build and the price the farmer will pay. This seems like a simple, two-person transaction in line with Smith's ideal. In reality, however, it is much more complex.

This stream is used by several other enterprises and individuals downriver. By damming the stream and substantially altering the volume or direction of the flow, farmer Jones and the contractor are significantly affecting others who were not directly parties to the transaction. These individuals and groups downstream may even be put out of business by what seemed like a simple transaction by the farmer and the contractor. These consequences often extend far beyond the parties of the original transaction, and they are present and important in many aspects of the U.S. economy.

The plain fact is that when one enters into some transactions, especially ones that affect the environment, there will likely be consequences for someone else who is not a direct party to the transaction. The resulting externalities can be severe, costly, and wide in impact, as when a plant dumps its manufacturing wastes into a body of water used for drinking or recreation by a large community. Or, they can be costly and severe, but limited to only a few, as when an individual buys the property next to your home and decides to open a commercial enterprise, which, because of noise, smell, dangerous emissions, or traffic, makes it difficult or impossible for you to use your home for residential purposes any longer.

The real problem is that competing uses of resources or property are often exclusive and nondivisible. The stream can either be used for damming and power upriver or it can be used for recreation or manufacturing downriver. It may not be possible for it to be used for both. Farmer Jones and his contractor, in building that dam, are making the ultimate decision on the use of that resource for all potential consumers. You want to use your property as a residence for your family. Your neighbor wants to use his property as a business concern. The uses are incompatible. If he operates his business next door to you, you may no longer be able to use your property as a residence. Your neighbor's use of his property the way he wants has precluded your using your property as you want. He has made the decision on how you will use your property.

Externalities are not always negative. One transaction may benefit the economic position of others not direct parties to the original transaction. You may own a vacant lot. On the vacant lot next to you a person decides to put up a small amusement park. This creates the need for parking and your lot may be used to serve this need, thereby increasing its value. Positive externalities are important and do provide additional opportunities stemming from the transactions of others. It is the serious, costly, and frequently negative externalities, however, that make it difficult for society to ignore the consequences of what may seem to be simple transactions between two parties, but which are, in reality, transactions with far-reaching implications for others not direct parties to the transaction. And because these externalities are often present, the exchanges between the initial buyer and seller, even though both may benefit by them, may not, as Smith hoped, work to the ultimate benefit of society.

Let me add a final note on the complexity of individual transactions and the difficulty in assuming they can work, as isolated exchanges, ultimately to benefit all. Smith imagined relatively small enterprises and small exchanges with limited consequences. A buyer or seller who made a bad deal would fail. This ability to fail is important, because it is a principal mechanism regulating market direction and evolution. These failures were important to the individual participant, but this failure was seen as having limited impact on society as a whole, except as a weederout of bad enterprises and thereby a positive contributor to society in general. Again, large, complex, interdependent modern society has made this position less tenable.

There are, quite simply, some enterprises that are so important, so broadly entrenched in economic and social life, so important to national defense or national identity, that it is really not credible that they could be allowed to fail. Even if a failure is due to inherent weaknesses, rather than uncontrollable external occurrences, the failing enterprise may be linked so closely to other important, nonfailing enterprises and general social and economic well-being that citizens and their governments will not, and should not, let it fail. The federal government's loan guarantees to Chrysler Corporation are one example. The importance of maintaining the jobs in this industry and all those related directly and indirectly to it led the government to at least try to help Chrysler become competitive again. The plan worked, Chrysler became a more profitable corporation, employment at Chrysler and in its related suppliers and distribution networks was maintained, and large sections of the country were saved from serious unemployment and economic decline.

Economist Lester Thurow has discussed the problem of protecting against such large corporate failures:

> The growth of large economic institutions also forces government to take many protective actions. At the heart of capitalism and competitive markets lies the doctrine of failure. The inefficient are to be driven out of business by the efficient. But governments cannot tolerate the failure of large economic actors. Neither the Lockheed Corporation nor New York City can be allowed to fail, since the disruptions to our integrated economy would be too large to tolerate. Needed military goods would not be delivered, and millions of bondholders would lose a substantial part of their wealth. In both cases, the rescue was organized by a conservative, free-market, Republican government. Any other government would have done the same.[11]

Thurow has pointed out that when the reality of failure on such a grand scale looms, even conservative, free-market decision makers realize the need for positive governmental intervention.

EFFECTIVE CONTRACT-ENFORCEMENT MECHANISM

For market exchanges to be acceptable as the central driving force in a society's economic life, then proper contract-enforcement mechanisms are essential. This is so for two reasons. First, both parties in an exchange must be able to hold the other party to the basic timing, quantity, and price agreements reached. If the selling party promises to deliver a specific amount of a product or service at a particular time and for a specified price, then the buyer must have confidence, even beyond the promise of the provider, that consequences can be imposed and recompense received if the product or service is not delivered as promised. And, by the same token, the seller or service provider must be confident that the consumer will pay the fee as specified and if not, that a mechanism exists to force compliance. Second, the consuming party must be confident in the quality of the product or service delivered. This may not be obvious until long after the product or service is delivered and the fee has been paid. This is because, for much of what one buys, product or service quality is not immediately observable at the point of the sale, but can be determined only after some period of use.

For Smith and present-day conservatives, the appropriate enforcement mechanism is litigation—civil court action to recover damages or enforce contractual agreements. The unhappy buyer or seller simply sues the other party to enforce the explicit and implicit terms of the exchange agreement. This looks very good at first glance. Government, through its operation of the courts and not through other more direct regulatory mechanisms, provides the forum and enforcement power to guarantee that all parties to a transaction live up to their side of the bargain. If they do not, the courts will surely see that they pay the price for their failure.

While this simple scenario may sound good in the abstract, its reality falls quite short of expectations in modern society. This failure occurs for three simple reasons. The first takes us back to our earlier point on the inadequacy of proper information. This lack of information is especially troubling for consumers when they try to identify the specific nature of a problem and tie it to a particular provider. Suppose you have a new roof put on your house. The shingle seller guarantees the product for 15 years. The contractor installing the roof guarantees his work for 5 years. Two years after the roof has been installed and paid for, leaking begins to occur, and shingles fall off the roof. Does the problem lie in some natural occurrence relating not to product or installation but to weather and the elements? Have you had particularly windy or rainy weather that might have affected even the best-quality and best-installed roof? Is there a structural flaw in the design of your house? Is the basic problem in the material itself, indicating that the company selling you the shingles or the manufacturer selling the shingles to it is at fault? Or did the installer do something to damage the roof or fail to do something that could have prevented the roof damage?

The homeowner will have great difficulty sorting out these possibilities and identifying who, if anyone, in the exchange with him has failed to live up to his side of the bargain. The example I have provided is a simple one. We all know what roofs are and what shingles are supposed to do. Compared with many of the market exchanges we engage in, this one is remarkably simple. Yet even in this simple exchange, the proper, court-enforced recourse for the consumer is difficult to discern. The information needed to begin the process of recovery is difficult and perhaps very expensive to obtain.

Let us suppose, however, that you either had the time and skill or had the money to buy the time and skill needed to sort out the specific deficiency in your roof. You know who is at fault and take him to court to enforce the warranty under which you agreed to the original transaction. Now you are facing the

Table 5.3
Age of Civil Cases Pending in U.S. District Courts, 1976–1985

Year	Total	Less than 1 Year	1 to 2 Years	2 to 3 Years	3 Years and Over
1976	149,618	57%	25%	10%	7.5%
1977	163,798	55	24	12	9
1978	173,827	54	23	11	11
1979	183,625	56	22	11	12
1980	186,958	58	22	10	10
1981	196,646	60	22	9	9
1982	217,623	62	21	9	8
1983	246,863	63	21	9	7
1984	246,632	61	22	9	7.5
1985	251,177	62	21	9	8

Source: <u>Federal Judicial Workload Statistics</u>. Administrative Office of the United States Courts, Statistical Analysis and Reports Division, December 31, 1985, pp. 13–14.

second problem confronting consumers in using litigation as the basic market enforcement mechanism: the problem of the adequacy of the court system properly to enforce market exchange. The term "proper" is an appropriate one here. For enforcement to be effective, it must be both timely and accessible to most buyers and sellers. Here the conservative, free-market ideal runs into serious problem, for the court system is neither timely nor accessible.

Litigation is a very expensive and time-consuming process. The cost for the lawyers, investigators, and other case-related personnel and services one needs to contest anything but a trivial case is staggering. And, if you have a trivial case like the roof example we used earlier, you will have difficulty finding affordable legal assistance to help present your case. The settlement one is likely to receive from the roof case could not begin to pay any reputable lawyer for the time he or she might invest in winning your case for you. So most lawyers will simply advise you not to pursue action at all. If, however, you persist and insist on a trial to recover your loss and enforce your original exchange, you will then find that court dockets are extremely crowded and that it may take months or years for the courts to reach resolution of your case.

Table 5.3 shows the age of civil cases pending in U.S. district courts from 1976 to 1985. These delays refer to district-court outcomes only. They do not take into account additional delays resulting from any appeals that are pursued, nor do they take into account the fact that many of these cases may have begun in state courts and after action (or inaction) there, been transferred to federal court. While a majority of district-court cases seem to be completed in one year or less, nearly 40 percent of all cases take more than a year to reach closure. And large numbers of cases take two, three, or more years to complete just the district-court action. Similar delays face most state-court systems.[12] Additional appeals increase both the time and costs of litigation, and the tremendous increase in cases from 1976 to 1985 shows how much of our nation's resources are being diverted away from productive economic enterprise and into protracted and often indecisive court action. The upshot of all thesse cases, in terms of expense and time is that few, except relatively well-off buyers and sellers, can successfully use the court system to enforce their market exchanges. And even for these more privileged competitors, the time and cost involved to correct a problem calls into question the adequacy of litigation as an effective, efficient, or timely regulator and enforcer of the free-market process.

The final problem of using litigation as the principal regulator and enforcer of market exchanges is that its "protections" are generally *ex post facto* in nature. The damage or wrong has usually already been done. The court process merely provides later recompense for this failure. In many important instances, however, *ex post facto* justice of this kind is largely irrelevant to the wronged party. If I purchase and consume a product that I believe to be safe and it seriously harms me or even kills me, the fact that my heirs may be able to receive some recompense for my injury is little comfort to me. What I really needed was some protection earlier on to prevent the injury from occurring. In a highly complex economy like ours, with a myriad of potentially dangerous products, foods, drugs, and services, consumers seem little comforted by the thought that perhaps, if their injury can be determined and if costly litigations can be won, they or their heirs may be able to recover something from the death or injury to them or another loved one. The public should not have to, and will not stand for such an *ex post facto* regulatory mechanism.

The preceding discussion has shown that while Smith's free-market solution may have been appropriate to the smaller-scale and less-complex world he inhabited in 1760, it is much less appropriate for the modern U.S. economy. The underlying conditions that must be present for Smith's design to work effectively—information, competition, simple exchanges, and adequate enforcement—are much less appropriate to today's market exchanges. There is a final point, however, which neither Smith nor his present-day disciples have discussed, that must be remembered when relying on self-regulating market exchanges to allocate goods and services for society. This is the crucial question of the initial distribution of resources that one brings to the marketplace.

As we discussed in earlier chapters, many potential participants in the market have, because of discrimination or other environmental constraints, substantially fewer resources with which to compete in the economic game than do others.

If the marketplace is to be the principal allocator of goods and services, then one cannot avoid the question of access to that competition. The terrible fact, in Smith's time and our own, is that many, through no fault of their own, simply do not have the resources to compete, either as buyers or sellers. The resulting allocation is flawed, therefore, because many might have made other choices, which might have directed society and the economy in other ways if they had resources to participate in the process. And, even if they can be assumed to make choices similar to their more prosperous neighbors, the fact that they cannot participate in the game limits the legitimacy of the process to claim appropriateness as the ultimate arbiter of a nation's social and economic life.

THE ROLE OF GOVERNMENT IN ECONOMIC DEVELOPMENT

The early realization, largely intuitive, perhaps, of limits in the array of economic activities that were truly market organized led U.S. citizens and elected officials to seek active government participation in the economy to support and control various economic activities. All levels of government—federal, state, and local—sought, as early as the 1800s, to encourage, promote, and regulate various economic enterprises. These activities were usually seen and justified as promoting much-needed economic development. In the nineteenth century, taking advantage of America's federalism system and the freedom granted to states to regulate many activities, states actively engaged in economic regulation and promotion, including state licensing and tax laws that were designed to give advantages to local enterprises over out-of-state competitors.[13] In the competition to attract settlers, capital, entrepreneurs, and labor, "federalism served one of the preeminent needs of the 19th century. It encouraged the states to use corporate franchises and monopolies, land grants, tax incentives, and a host of other inducements to stimulate economic growth."[14]

In seeking to take advantage of the economic growth that could come from being on a railroad line and participating in the cattle trade, civic leaders and elected officials in hundreds of towns like Ellsworth, Kansas, petitioned state and national governments for competitive advantages and granted rights and privileges to private enterprises to increase their chances of success in promoting economic development.[15] "Towns as well as states competed in countless ways. At the state level taxes, usury laws, and corporate charters were used to attract business. . . . Communities—each a budding New York or Boston in the eyes of adoring boosters—vied with each other for factories, public buildings, post offices, and land offices, but most of all for new roads, canals, and rail lines."[16]

Citizens sought public works as a principal vehicle for development, and laws protecting corporations involved in such work and allowing eminent domain were welcomed. These nineteenth-century American citizens, businessmen, and government officials were not waiting for the marketplace to bring them the economic development they sought as the source of a better life. They were actively using all levels of government to facilitate such development.

This free-wheeling, relatively unabashed, very direct intervention of governments in the economic life of nineteenth-century America partially yielded, in the twentieth century, to another more indirect form of regulation and promotion. Independent regulatory commissions, like the Interstate Commerce Commission, were established to help "control" the activities of the very entities governments had just helped become so strong. The Interstate Commerce Commission, for example, "was created to keep railroads' freight rates and passenger fares low."[17] The stated goals of this agency and many other federal and state government regulatory agencies in the early twentieth century were to combat bigness, encourage competition, facilitate access, and protect consumer interests. Whether they did this very well and whether they helped or hurt citizens and the viability of economic enterprises in the United States is often debated. Many argue that they were shameful protectors of clientele industries and hurt both competition and consumers. Whatever their legacy to U.S. economic life, the important point, for our purposes here, is that these regulatory/supportive activities were another example of citizens' attempts to use government and not to depend slavishly on market forces to direct economic activity.

A very creative and successful plan of government intervention to facilitate and regulate economic activity was to come in the pre- and post-World War II period. At this time, the importance of technology in economic development and national security had become clear. To prosper in this new technological age would require new ideas and the ability to take these new ideas to the marketplace. The importance of education and research became especially clear, and governments, both state and national, saw the need to facilitate both of these important elements now undergirding economic development and national security.

State and national governments had a successful model to follow in building the infrastructure needed to develop the new technological economy. This model was the extensive government support provided to agriculture, beginning in the late 1800s and continuing into the twentieth century. Through massive infusion of education, research, and extension funds, state and federal governments provided a technological revolution in agricultural production that made U.S. agriculture the productivity and technological leader in this economic sector. The abundance of agricultural products present in the world today is due, largely, to production techniques and other advances (seeds, breeding programs, nutrients, herbicides, insecticides, planting-rotation schemes, and so on) developed in the United States with substantial state and federal government assistance.

One of the major problems our farmers face today—the world surpluses that have driven down prices and reduced exports and farm incomes—is directly related to our successful technological revolution in agricultural production. We are a victim of our own success. Through the export of the superior agricultural technology we developed with substantial government support, we have helped our competitors who, with lower labor costs and government subsidies and protectionist policies, can now produce much of the food they once purchased from us and also export their own surpluses to compete with ours in world markets.

Building on their successful agricultural model, state and federal governments knew what to do to foster economic development in the more technologically based world of the 1930s and beyond: Invest in education, invest in research, and provide a market for the products of early market entrants. And this is exactly the strategy adopted by the national government and supported by supplemental activities of the states. During this crucial period of the 1930s to the 1950s, the national government became an active participant in the development of some of the most important industries of the modern economy. Below is a brief sketch of the government's role in the development of some of these important industries: aviation, semiconductors and computers, and pharmaceuticals.

Aviation

The national government, through governmental agencies directly stimulating and assisting aircraft design, through research and development funds, and through its procurement policies, played a major role in the successful evolution of the U.S. aircraft industry. "Aviation is an industry where, from the beginning, a strong national security interest has spilled over to facilitate the development of civil aircraft as well as military."[18] In an extensive analysis of the commerical aircraft industry, Mowery and Rosenberg point out the crucial role actions of the national government played in developing a strong civil aviation industry in the United States.

The commercial aircraft industry has reaped considerable benefits as a technological "borrower." Many of the significant innovations in commercial aircraft design, including many incorporated in the DC–3 (the first great commercial success in the industry), were originally developed by manufacturers of airframes and engines for military applications. . . .

The impressive record of innovation exhibited by the commercial aircraft industry reflects the industry's good fortune as a beneficiary of at least three important external sources of innovation and/or research support; innovations in other industries, such as metallurgy or electronics, government-supported research in civil aviation, and military procurement and research support.[19]

Through government agencies like the National Advisory Committee on Aeronautics (later to evolve into NASA), through substantial research and development funds, and through military procurement and research and development policies, the national government has been a significant player in this very important industry.

Semiconductors and Computers

The semiconductor industry and the related computer industry also benefited greatly from early government support and investment, although, when compared to aviation, the role of private firms is more central and important in these areas. In a comprehensive examination of the development of the semiconductor industry, Levin has argued;

Since the end of World War II, the U.S. government has devoted substantial funds to semiconductor research and development. The bulk of these funds, especially in the early years, came from the military services, but support has come also from NASA, the National Bureau of Standards, and the National Science Foundation. . . . Of the various policy instruments that have directly or indirectly influenced the evolution of semiconductor technology, none has been of such fundamental importance as public procurement of electronic components and systems for purposes of national defense and space exploration.[20]

Governmental activity related to computer development is somewhat more direct than that provided to semiconductors. At the very earliest stages of development of the computer, the federal government assisted in planning, funding, sponsoring information exchanges, and being a ready and supportive market. Various agencies of the federal government participated in these crucial, early stages in the development of computer technology—the Census Bureau, the Bureau of Standards, the Office of Naval Research, and many other agencies of the Department of Defense. "Government-sponsored research played a key role in the emergence of the transistor. In the 1930's, and especially during the war, Bell Labs and various universities and industrial companies became involved in a variety of governmentally sponsored projects related to crystal detectors. The work on radar in the late 1930's falls into this category. The link between radar and computers is important."[21]

The federal government, through research and development contracts and by standing as a principal and dependable purchaser of computers, helped the early computer companies get established and remain viable. Katz and Phillips point out the incredible importance of these early government programs in support of computer development. "Until at least 1951–1954, all significant aspects of R&D were government funded. . . . The first attempts at commercialization were essentially by-products of projects that directly or indirectly were motivated by governmental interests and governmental funding."[22]

Pharmaceuticals

The pattern of government assistance to the pharmaceutical industry is similar in one way to that for computers and semiconductors, in that the government, through various agencies and programs, invested heavily in health-related re-

Table 5.4
Expenditures on Health R&D (billions of dollars)

Year	Total Health R&D	Federal Health R&D	Private Drug R&D
1960	.9	.4	.2
1965	1.9	1.2	.3
1970	2.8	1.7	.5
1975	4.6	2.8	.8
1978	6.2	3.8	1.1

Source: U.S. Department of HEW, 1979 NIH *Almanac; PMA Factbook,* reprinted from Henry G. Grabowski and J. M. Vernon, "The Pharmaceutical Industry," in *Government and Technical Progress,* ed. Richard R. Nelson (New York: Pergamon, 1982), p. 306.

search and development. Table 5.4 shows the relative importance of this crucial federal investment. As the data indicate, during the very important period of drug developmentt, the 1960s to the 1980s, federal health R&D was substantially greater than that undertaken by private companies. And when one adds the substantial investment by state universities in basic research in related areas, the fact emerges that massive federal and state government investment in this area has provided much of the intellectual capital on which drug and genetic engineering advances are based.

In addition to this significant level of general R&D investment, government policies have also helped in the development of specific drugs and technologies. An important example is the role of the British and U.S. governments' investments and assistance in the discoveries needed to mass-produce penicillin during World War II.[23] And although government labs have not been major direct developers of specific new drugs in most disease areas, tending to focus on basic research discoveries on which such new drugs are based, they have been very active in cancer-drug development. Grabowski and Vernon report that "Congress dramatically increased the budget of the National Cancer Institute for new drug development during the past decade. The annual budget in this respect, now over 200 million dollars annually, is larger than the total R&D budget of any of the major U.S. pharmaceutical firms."[24] It is hoped that a similar government R&D investment in AIDS research will lead to drug advances that can help prevent or control this deadly disease. And as the AIDS crisis has demonstrated, it is the government, not private companies, who are the focal point for citizens and health providers as they seek protection from this advancing problem. In areas as important as life and death, few seem willing to rely on markets and profit incentives to provide a timely or adequate solution to important and acute problems.

In all of these economic areas, as in agriculture before them, the successful U.S. pattern has been a partnership between the public and private sectors. While dreams of a free market as the mainspring of economic success may be widespread among conservatives, our successful reality has been a mixed economy, with significant contributions coming from both the public and private sectors. This symbiotic relationship has not been without conflict and has often produced results less than expected or desired, but it has led us to substantial economic success over a time span unequaled by any other country.

CONCLUSION

According to conservative ideology and dogma, government is the principal enemy of freedom. This position was summarized very clearly by William Simon, former secretary of the treasury under Presiden Nixon and a forceful conservative spokesman. On returning from a visit to the USSR, he reports feeling "it is only when one confronts political tyranny that one really grasps the meaning and importance of freedom. What I actually realized in Air Force Two is that 'freedom' is difficult to understand because it isn't a presence but an absence—an absence of governmental constraints."[25] The free market, unrestricted by government, is for conservatives like Simon the greatest economic and social freedom possible. They believe what Adam Smith told them, that an unregulated market is the best, most efficient, and most equitable allocator of resources in society.

The problem for conservatives is that there are many obstacles to freedom, that government is not always one of them, and that market behavior often is. In the United States, government is not the monolith Simon saw in the USSR. Here we have many levels of government and, as our founding fathers designed, one level may actually protect us not only from social and economic evils but from the evils perpetrated by other levels of government. We have seen the oppressive and discriminatory behavior of southern whites toward their black fellow citizens for much of the past 200 years. It took strong and decisive action from government, the national one, to help correct this substantial political, social and economic injustice.

And, not only is it true that government is not always the enemy of freedom; it is equally true that free markets are not always friends of freedom. As we saw in this chapter, there are many weaknesses and shortcomings in the market model described by Smith, which make it much less than perfectly applicable to modern U.S. society. Discrimination, prejudice, and non-merit-based inequalities in society often make the economic game an unfair one right from the beginning. Many may not have the resources to compete fairly and equally in the conservatives "noble struggle" for personal gain. And many of the exchanges, which Smith felt would produce so much good for all society, in fact benefit only the specific buyers and sellers, while, because of externalities, the rest of us may be suffering the consequences of their profitable exchange. As farmer Jones and the dam builder illustrated in our earlier example, market exchanges can be powerful limiters of the freedom of others. In market exchanges, the only morality is profit. It is not always—or only—government from which we need protection.

I agree with conservatives that we have accomplished much economically in this country and that we have much to be proud of, but these accomplishments have not come about because we have adhered to any absolutist, free-market ideal. Rather, our economic success is the result of a mixture of market action and government action—a mixed economy. What our own successful history has shown us is that we need a pragmatic, nonideological approach to the problem of balancing regulation and competition. We have seen that these are very complex issues. It is simply not very helpful to begin with an immovable ideological position and then deduce that no government regulation is ever appropriate. Such an ideological base is, as I have demonstrated, flawed from a number of perspectives. There are situations when markets cannot and do not work well in modern society, and there are times when regulation is useful and helpful. We must look at each situation and judge whether or not the role of government is needed and appropriate, not simply assume, *a priori,* that it cannot be.

NOTES

1. See, for example, conservative spokesmen like Milton and Rose Friedman, *Free To Choose* (New York: Avon, 1980); George Gilder, *Wealth and Poverty* (New York: Bantam Books, 1981); Irving Kristol, *Two Cheers for Capitalism* (New York: New American Library, 1978); and William E. Simon, *A Time for Truth* (New York: Reader's Digest Press, 1978).

2. Friedman, *Free To Choose*, p. 5.

3. *Austin American Statesman*, July 4, 1987, p. 4.

4. James A. Davis and T. W. Smith, *General Social Surveys, 1972–1986* (Chicago: National Opinion Research Center, 1986), p. 358.

5. Davis and Smith, *Surveys*, p. 364–65.

6. Davis and Smith, *Surveys*, p. 365–66.

7. Davis and Smith, *Surveys*, p. 366.

8. Robert L. Heilbroner, *The Worldly Philosophers*, 4th ed. (New York: Simon & Schuster, 1972), pp. 57, 60.

9. Kristol, *Two Cheers*, p. xii, 9.

10. U.S. Bureau of the Census, *Statistical Abstract of the United States 1987*, 107th ed. (Washington, DC, 1986), pp. 374, 375, 507, 519, 522; and *Fortune*, April 27, 1987, pp. 359–61.

11. Lester C. Thurow, *The Zero Sum Society* (New York: Penguin Books, 1981), pp. 21–22.

12. See National Center for State Courts, *State Court Caseload Statistics Annual Report 1985*, December 1987.

13. Donald J. Pisani, "Promotion and Regulation: Constitutionalism and the American Economy," *Journal of American History* 74:3 (December 1987); 744–45.

14. Pisani, "Promotion and Regulation," p. 744.

15. Robert R. Dykstra, *The Cattle Towns* (New York: Atheneum, 1970).

16. Pisani, "Promotion and Regulation," p. 745.

17. Louis M. Kohlmeier, Jr., *The Regulators* (New York: Harper & Row, 1969), pp. 145–46.

18. Richard R. Nelson, "Public Policy and Technical Progress: A Cross-Industry Analysis," in *Government and Technical Progress,* ed. Richard R. Nelson (New York: Pergamon Press, 1982), p. 6.

19. David C. Mowery and Nathan Rosenberg, "The Commercial Aircraft Industry," in Nelson, *Government and Technical Process,* pp. 103, 125.

20. Richard C. Levin, "The Semiconductor Industry," in Nelson, *Government and Technical Progress,* pp. 57–58, 66.

21. Barbara G. Katz and Almarin Phillips, "The Computer Industry," in Nelson, *Government and Technical Progress,* p. 199.

22. Katz and Phillips, "Computer Industry," p. 211.

23. NOVA, "The Rise of a Wonder Drug," Public Broadcasting Service, March 18, 1986. For information on penicillin and for a more general discussion of the positive role government had in this health area, see Edward Shorter, *The Health Century* (New York: Doubleday, 1987).

24. Henry G. Grabowski and J. M. Vernon, "The Pharmaceutical Industry," in Nelson, *Government and Technical Progress,* p. 352.

25. Simon, *A Time for Truth,* p. 19.

6

Where Have All the Programs Gone?

Governmental policies and programs are the mechanisms used by societies to initiate and direct collective activities needed to achieve societal goals that would not be achieved through private actions alone. The maintenance of law and order, providing for defense against external threats, addressing pressing health problems, and providing mass education are only a few examples of the myriad activities that citizens of most nations expect their governments, through the organization of collective efforts, to provide for them. The organization of these collective efforts usually requires that resources of money, property, and personnel be diverted by governments from certain activities, individuals, and groups to others. These diversions are usually controversial, because different groups give and receive disparate amounts of resources. People will, therefore, naturally disagree over what they want and need from government actions for themselves, what they want to provide to other citizens, and how much they are willing to pay for these government activities.

One of the most controversial sets of government diversion policies lies in the area of social welfare. Through a number of programs and policies providing direct and in-kind benefits, the various levels of government in the United States have redirected resources to selected beneficiary groups. Through their taxing powers, national, state and local governments have collected money from all citizens to be used to provide social-welfare programs to select groups of citizens. These programs range from those principally the responsibility of the federal government, like Social Security and Medicare, through federal–state partnership programs like Medicaid and Aid to Families with Dependent Children (AFDC), to federally assisted state and local programs like charity hospitals, orphanages, and facilities for the mentally and physically handicapped.

There is a fair degree of consensus among Americans that programs that serve groups truly in need are an appropriate exercise of government power. There is not a great deal of consensus, however, over which groups are truly needy, which programs are the most effective, or how much money should be diverted for these purposes. Ideological dogmas, often selected and screened by perceived self-interest, play a key role in influencing citizen decisions on the proper role of government as resource diverter and provider. As we have seen in earlier chapters, conservatives tend to feel that being in need is primarily the result of personal inadequacies, not environmental factors and constraints. Therefore, conservative solutions to the problems of need tend to revolve around personal, not governmental actions. Conservatives tend to view few as truly needy and, as a result of this belief, tend to support limited government expenditures on behalf of those identified as needy by definitions other than their own.

In addition to this basic ideological predisposition opposing extensive social-welfare programs, conservatives take great solace in pointing out their belief that such programs seldom work and often create more problems than they solve. In making these assertions, they have moved beyond the realm of ideological discussion and advocacy into the very different world of empirical observation. The two should not be confused. It is not enough for ideological advocates, either liberal or conservative, to simply assert, on abstract theoretical grounds alone, that a program does or does not work. It is not enough to present shallow, selected ''evidence'' to simply overlay a fundamentally ideologically based argument. Individuals genuinely concerned about these issues need to look at our desires for ourselves and our fellow citizens and honestly evaluate programs in the light of what they actually do, what resources they actually have at their disposal, and what reasonable people could actually expect them to accomplish. What, then, are conservatives saying about the record of social-welfare programs, what empirical evidence are they presenting to bolster their case, and how well does this argument stand up against a broad investigation of the data available on the impact of social-welfare programs on the U.S. society?

The general position of conservative spokesmen, from President Reagan on down, regarding the impact of social-welfare programs is that at best they have been ineffective and at worst they have been pernicious. In his 1986 State of the Union Address, President Reagan lashed out at the broken social dreams of Americans and the failure of programs that have created a ''spider's web of dependency. . . . After hundreds of billions of dollars in poverty programs, the plight of the poor grows more painful. But the waste in dollars and cents pales before the most tragic loss: the sinful waste of human spirit and potential.''[1] The charge by the president and his conservative fellows is a simple one—that after spending huge sums of money we have only exacerbated, not alleviated, poverty in the United States.

To support these basic assertions, conservatives point to general social and economic data and specific program-evaluation data. Let us first look at the general data that conservatives are presenting to support their case of overall program failure.

GENERAL TRENDS 1965–80: LOSING GROUND, HOLDING GROUND, OR GAINING GROUND

Perhaps the most comprehensive and extensive compilation of data purporting to support the conservative position of the negative impact of social-welfare spending on the incidence of poverty over the past 20 years is Charles Murray's book, *Losing Ground*.[2] Underwritten by the conservative Manhattan Institute and publicized through their efforts,[3] this book has become the data bible for conservatives' attacks on the social-welfare programs designed and implemented in the 1960s and 1970s. While Murray makes both general-level and specific-program attacks in this book, this section will focus on his general-level assertions.

In presenting his case, Murray raises a very simple question for his readers: If all these welfare programs had been working properly, should we not expect to see poverty substantially reduced between 1965 and today? Then he goes on to point out that not only did improvements not occur, but that the poor actually lost ground after the implementation of these programs. To bolster his points, Murray presents a lot of macro-level trend data comparing poverty rates from the 1950s to 1980.

Readers need to keep two thoughts in mind as they evaluate the relevance of the data Murray presents to the conclusions he draws. The first is that statistics, or the data on which they are based, are inherently neither right or wrong, good or bad. One can gather many different kinds of data related to the same topic and array them in many different ways to arrive at many different types of conclusions. The only real check on the "correctness" of a specific array of data is its logical relevance to the fundamental issue under study. The second thought to remember is that the fact that two observations or events are associated together in time does not constitute proof that the two events are causally related. They may be totally unrelated and simply randomly juxtaposed in time, or they may both be caused by some other, nonmeasured variable, and not really directly related to each other. Keeping these thoughts in mind, let us look at the principal data Murray presents to make his argument that in spite of increased program activity, the lot of the poor is worse today than it was before the programs were implemented.

Murray presents the major data array essential to his spending and poverty thesis in a figure entitled "The Poverty/Spending Paradox."[4] In this figure Murray traces the total federal cash expenditures for assistance programs and the numbers of persons below the official poverty line from 1950 to 1980. The data Murray used were reported in the Appendix of his book and are shown in

Table 6.1
Federal Cash Assistance and Persons beneath the Poverty Level, 1950–1980

Year	Cash Public Assistance (1,000,000s)	N	Total Persons in Poverty %
1950	3744		30.2
1951	3760		28.0
1952	3752		27.9
1953	4184		26.2
1954	4301		27.9
1955	4426		24.5
1956	4429		22.9
1957	4703		22.8
1958	4791		23.1
1959	5144	39490	22.4
1960	5158	39851	22.2
1961	5333	39628	21.9
1962	5645	38625	21.0
1963	5971	36436	19.5
1964	6236	36055	19.0
1965	6465	33185	17.3
1966	7107	30424	15.7
1966r		28510	14.7
1967	7663	27769	14.2
1968	8252	25389	12.8
1969	9218	24147	12.1
1970	9458	25420	12.6
1971	11644	25559	12.5
1972	12483	24460	11.9
1973	12414	22973	11.1
1974	13577	24260	11.6
1974r		23370	11.2
1975	15800	25877	12.3
1976	15274	24975	11.8
1977	16101	24720	11.6
1978	15525	24497	11.4
1979	14528	25345	11.6
1979r		26072	11.7
1980	14260	29272	13.0

Source: Data presented in this Table derived from U.S. Government figures reported in Charles Murray, Losing Ground, Appendix Tables 3 and 5, pp. 243 and 245.

Table 6.1. On the basis of the data reported in this table, Murray argues that major gains in reducing poverty occurred before the War on Poverty in 1965:

After two decades of reasonable steady progress, improvement slowed in the late sixties and stopped altogether in the seventies. The proportion dipped to its low point, 11 percent, in 1973. A higher proportion of the American population was officially poor in 1980 than at any time since 1967. . . . The number of people living in poverty stopped declining just as the public-assistance program budgets and the rate of increase in those budgets were highest. The question is why this should be.[5]

This is an excellent question. Murray wants us to believe that the programs implemented in the 1960s and 1970s stifled initiative and exacerbated dependency in such ways as to increase the numbers of Americans living below the poverty line. There are other, perhaps more appropriate, interpretations of the data presented in Table 6.1.

First, let us look at the data themselves. What exactly is Murray presenting to us with these figures? The cash public-assistance figures he reports include Social Security benefits, which make up the bulk of the assistance measured by Murray. Few would argue that most of these Social Security benefit increases are received by the hard-core poor, so it is hard to agree with Murray and others who want us to believe that these expanded federal outlays led to decreased efforts by the poor. Ellwood and Summers point out that "between 1970 and 1980, cash assistance expenditures [for the nonelderly] rose from $13.7 billion to $18.9 billion. Yet over the entire decade, annual expenditures per nonelderly poor person rose just $93."[6] The change in cash-assistance benefits measured by Murray cannot be expected to be associated with increases in the economic status of the hard-core nonelderly poor after 1970, because, in reality, the actual increase in cash-assistance payments was essentially nonexistent.

This problem with the relatively flat level of cash-assistance benefits to the nonelderly poor after 1970 and its obvious lack of impact on their poverty rate point out a second problem with Murray's presentation. Many of the benefits that the poor receive are in-kind, not cash, transfers—food stamps, housing allowances, medical services. These in-kind expenditures did increase during the 1960s and 1970s and have had an important impact on the level of poverty among the elderly and nonelderly poor. When one looks at these in-kind social-welfare expenditures together with the cash ones arrayed in Murray's figure, the "success rate" of the poverty programs takes on quite a different cast. According to Murray's own figures, the "net poverty rate," the poverty figures, taking cash and in-kind transfers into consideration, dropped from over 12 percent of the population in 1965 to 6.2 percent in 1972.[7]

Rather than marvel at the reduction in poverty in-kind transfers accomplished between 1965 and 1972, Murray would prefer to concentrate on the post–1972 period, arguing that between 1972 and 1979, when in-kind assistance doubled, the poverty rate moved only to 6.1 percent. Here is proof positive that "huge increases in expenditures coincided with an end to progress."[8] While he is careful to use the term "coincided," remember that the thesis of Murray's book is that it is the programs themselves that have arrested progress.

This assertion of Murray's is not only difficult to substantiate, it flies in the face of 20 years of empirical poverty research that consistently has identified another, more obvious variable as the principal factor rapidly accelerating or deflating poverty levels in the United States. This crucial variable is the robustness of the economy. When levels of employment and inflation and their corollary—real family income—are favorable, poverty rates go down.[9] As Ellwood and Summers have demonstrated so clearly, "almost all of the variation in the poverty rate is tracked by movements in median family income. The poverty rate, and the poverty line as a fraction of total family income, move almost completely together."[10]

Government social-welfare programs exist within a general economic climate. Good programs in bad economic times may help reduce the rate of poverty increase generated by the overall economy, and good programs in good economic times may accelerate the process of poverty reduction generated by the overall strength of the economy. And it is conceivable that programs could be so bad as to accelerate poverty rates in bad times and retard them in good times. While the trend lines of Ellwood and Summers indicate that the latter is unlikely, a closer examination of Murray's data indicate that that is definitely not what is happening in his examples.

In Table 6.1 we see that if Murray had used 1979 as his end point rather than 1980, there would be four million less in poverty, a reduction of nearly 14 percent from the 1980 figure, a much more favorable comparison with the starting point of 1965. The jump in people in poverty from 1979 to 1980 was the largest single-year jump in the post–1965 period. What happened between 1979 and 1980? Was this the critical year when the accumulated evils of all those governmental programs finally burst loose into a frenzy of dependency? Such a scenario hardly seems likely, yet only such an explanation will support Murray's basic thesis of programs causing poverty increases. What did happen from 1979 to 1980, then, that could have had such a profound impact on the number of Americans falling under the poverty threshold? The answer that 20 years of poverty research tells us to expect was the recession of 1980 and the concomitant reduction in employment and earnings that drove the marginal nonpoor under the poverty line. In 1979, 5.8 percent of the labor force were unemployed. In the recession of 1980 this figure jumps to 7.0 percent. And from 1979 to 1980, the net change in GNP growth for the United States was a negative 0.3 percent.[11] This was a bad time economically for Amercians, and for the hardest hit, the marginal nonpoor, was enough to push them over the line.

Now let us turn to Murray's second indictment of social-welfare programs, the leveling off of net poverty from 1972 to 1979. Murray argues that this leveling occurred at a time when benefits were rising most rapidly, further asserting that it was the programs themselves that arrested progress. There is little of merit in this argument of Murray's. First, overall social-welfare benefit levels did double, from a federal outlay of over $100 billion in 1972 to $263 billion in 1979,[12] but the bulk of these increases occurred in Social Security and Medicare, general nonpoor beneficiary programs. In-kind programs like housing did move from around $2 billion to over $5 billion in this period,[13] but when compared to the Social Security and Medicare expenditures for the aged, they are small in level and therefore in expected impact.

More important, however, than the general level of funding for the poor during this period is the general economic trend that was occurring at the same time. The period between 1972 and 1980 marks a serious downturn in the U.S. economy. While there was an occasional bright spot in one year or another, the general economic climate was quite negative during this period. In three of the years, 1973–74, 1974–75, and 1979–80, the rate of increase in GNP in constant dollars was actually negative, indicating a very sluggish and troubled economy.[14] Unemployment and family- and household-income measures of this period point out the same problem. While household median income growth in the first of the period, 1972, was a healthy 4.0 percent, it dropped to 2.1 percent in 1973, −4.0 percent in 1974, −3.4 percent in 1975, 1.6 percent in 1976, 0.5 percent in 1977, 3.1 percent in 1978, −1.8 percent in 1979, and −5.2 percent in 1980.[15] In most of the years Murray highlights, actual levels of family and household income in constant dollars were dropping sharply. Unemployment figures tell the same story. Unemployment rates began in 1972 at 5.5 percent, peaked in 1975 and 1976 at 8.3 percent and 7.6 percent, respectively, and ended in 1980 at 7 percent, well above the starting point.[16]

What all these figures clearly point to is a serious economic problem throughout the period 1972–80. These negative macro economic factors are what drive many people into poverty. Therefore, the significantly bad times occurring in the period Murray has selected to make his point actually tell us nothing about poverty exacerbation due to programs and program spending. Quite the contrary. They tell us the serious effects macro economic declines can have on the poor and marginally nonpoor. If even the slight increases in the program expenditures Murray so derides had not been present at this very difficult economic time, we would not have seen a leveling of the poverty rate; we would have seen a substantial increase in it. A more appropriate reading of the economic times faced by the poor during the 1972–80 period points up the positive impact program efforts had in preventing poverty rates from skyrocketing during this long period of economic decline.

Murray never succeeds in directly attributing poverty-rate increases to government programs. The coincidences he finds can be explained much more efficiently and effectively by the special selection of his measures and time periods and by the overpowering presence and importance of general economic trends. As the more appropriate measure, net poverty, indicates, substantial progress has been made in reducing or holding down poverty levels, even in relatively difficult economic times.

SPECIFIC PROGRAM IMPACTS 1965–80

In the previous discussion we have seen the aggregate picture of poverty in the United States during the post–1965 period. We have examined general trends in program expenditures and economic cycles and related them to overall numbers and proportions of individuals living below the poverty line. Such analyses are instructive for giving broad pictures of societal conditions, but they tell us little about the actual conditions under which poor and near-poor citizens were living. To really measure whether or not the poor are better off or worse off after social-program implementation, we must look beyond these general figures and examine the actual conditions of our poorer neighbors. Only then can we tell if their condition has improved or receded vis-à-vis the programs designed to assist them. Let us look, then, at the effects of five social-welfare program areas on the actual life situations and conditions of poor Americans: health and medical services, preschool education, housing, Aid to Families with Dependent Children (AFDC), and job training.

Health and Medical Services

Included in this program category are the specific health programs like Medicare and Medicaid and the much smaller, but health-related, nutritional programs like Food Stamps, School Lunch Program, Maternal & Child Health Program, and Women, Infants, and Children Program. Since 1965, the national and state governments have devoted billions of dollars to these programs aimed at improving the health status of our elderly, poor and nonpoor, and our nonelderly poor citizens. Just to give you an example of the magnitude of the effort and the increasing dollar amounts, Medicare expenditures increased from a little over $7 billion in 1970 to over $64 billion in 1984.[17]

In spite of this tremendous level of effort, Charles Murray chose not to look at health-care impacts in his book criticizing the post–1965 social-welfare effort. One would think that a program of this magnitude would have merited some attention from one purporting to tell us whether or not citizens were better or worse off as a result of government programs. One reason for the omission may be that if one wants to tell a tale of doom and gloom, one will want to avoid countervailing arguments. And countervailing arguments are exactly what one will get in measuring the significant improvement in the health status of the U.S. poor after the implementation of these programs. We will examine two areas of significant health gains, access to health care and health status. One can array any number of measures to indicate the relative health status and health-system access of consumers of health care. Two of the more telling are levels of infant mortality and physician visits.

Access. Health statisticians have been tracing the access of Americans to health care for the past 30 years. In their most recent report on access to health care in the United States, the Robert Wood Johnson Foundation summarizes the access of poor and nonpoor Americans from 1953 to 1986.[18] Although one expects the poor to have more health problems and need more physician visits than the nonpoor, the fact is that before the inception of the post–1965 health programs, the average yearly number of health-care visits by the poor and nonpoor were virtually the same, about 4.5 visits per year. After the implementation of the programs, low-income patients did begin to average more visits per year than the nonpoor, the gap peaking in 1970 at about 4.7 visits for the poor and 3.7 for the nonpoor. In 1963, only 55 percent of the poor saw a physician, compared with 70 and 65 percent, respectively, for high- and medium-income citizens;

this gap closed substantially by 1970, after the implementation of the new program.[19] Additional figures further point out the significant gains in physician access made as a result of the federal and state health programs. "The percentage of the aged who saw a physician at least once a year climbed from the pre-Medicare rate of 68 percent to 83 percent in 1984"[20]; "71 percent of low income women received medical attention in the first trimester of pregnancy in 1976, compared with only 58 percent in 1963[21]; by 1976, poor children averaged 65 percent more physician visits than in 1964."[22]

Health Status. It is difficult to measure what the actual benefit of going to a physician means for a person's overall health status. Intuitively, we suspect that going to a physician will help reduce acute conditions and perhaps prevent chronic ones with early diagnosis and treatment. Most doctors would certainly agree that this is so, but overall statistical measures of general health status and mortality may not change markedly if physician visits increase by one per year. Thus, improvement in the health of many citizens is difficult to disentangle from the myriad of other public health, social and physical factors that may act to increase or decrease longevity. A poor individual may get more relief from acute and chronic ailments and may lead a higher quality life as a result of more physician visits; but such benefits—while very important to the individual—may not show up in overall health statistics.

There is a general health statistic, however, the infant mortality rate—that can indicate whether improvements in health care are leading to significant improvements in health status in one very important segment of our population. With this measure one can see the direct, life-and-death relationship between health programs and individual well-being. "Infant mortality declined rapidly from 1935 to 1950. It then entered a period of fairly moderate decline between 1950 and 1960, and remained relatively stable until 1965. From a 1965 rate of 24.7 deaths per 1000 live births, the rate plummeted to 17.6 in 1973."[23] In the post–1965 era, then, a time when Murray is pointing out how much the poor were losing ground, the fact is that in one of the most important areas, health, the poor were making significant gains, gains that can, to a substantial degree, be credited to significant investments in the health and nutritional status of the poor.

One must be careful not to overstate these health gains of the poor, however. While clear advances in the health status of the poor were made during the post–1965 period, we must keep these efforts in proper perspective. A substantial majority of the health-care dollars invested in this period were not aimed at the nonelderly poor. The principal beneficiaries of most of these health dollars were the elderly, both poor and nonpoor. Medicare is an entitlement program, and its huge medical expenditures go to the enrolled aged, regardless of poverty status. And what many do not know is that the majority of Medicaid expenditures are also spent on the elderly. "AFDC adults and children on public assistance receive about one-fourth of all Medicaid payments, even though they represent more than one-half of all Medicaid recipients. . . . The emphasis upon the elderly, disabled, and medically needy is reflected in the concentration of Medicaid benefits on institutional services. About 70% of all Medicaid expenditures go for hospital and nursing home care."[24] Most of this is for the elderly poor, not the welfare types of whom Murray is so critical.

The positive side is that in spite of this relatively low commitment to non-elderly-poor health expenditures, significant health gains were achieved among this group, especially the very young. In a recent study, Copeland and Meier, using time-series analysis, found "both Medicaid and WIC had a significant negative impact on the infant-mortality rate for all infants. We estimated that these federal programs saved between 20,000 and 35,000 infants per year."[25] It is no surprise, then, that implicitly responding to Murray's charges, Copeland and Meier titled their article "Gaining Ground."

Housing

There were many programs that the national government continued or initiated in the post–1965 period to assist in providing housing opportunities to the public. These ranged from public-housing programs to construction, rental, and purchasing subsidies, to VA and FHA loan programs to Urban Development Action Grants and Community Development Block Grants, to tax deductions for home-mortgage interest and taxes. One important fact to remember about these programs is that, with the exception of the public-housing efforts, few of them restricted their benefits to or were specifically aimed at poor citizens. "It is important to recognize that improving the quality and affordability of housing for the poor are only two of the goals of federal housing policy. Other objectives include stimulating housing production and smoothing out cyclical swings in production; increasing home ownership, especially among the middle class; increasing housing opportunities for minorities and for those with special needs; promoting neighborhood preservation and revitalization; and stimulating employment."[26] As we will see later, conservative critics of the housing programs of this era have tended to ignore this reality.

While Charles Murray does not mention housing in his critique of the post–1965 social welfare programs, other conservatives have strongly attacked housing programs and, in approaches similar to Murray's, have charged them as failures and contributors to the negative condition of the poor. One such conservative has, like Murray, written a major attack on the social programs of the 1960s and 1970s. This is Allen Matusow, whose book, *The Unraveling of America,*[27] is, like Murray's *Losing Ground,* a broad-based, negative assault on many of the programs of the post–1965 era. Like Murray, Matusow examines many of the programs of the period and finds them at best, wanting, and at worst, harmful.

One of the many program areas Matusow casts his gaze on is housing. Focusing almost exclusively on Sections 235 and 236 of the Housing and Urban Development Act of 1968, Matusow finds little good to say about the post–1965 housing policies. These two sections of the 1968 act provided mortgage-insurance assistance and cash payments to help low- and moderate-income home purchasers

(Sec. 235) and similar assistance for those seeking multifamily rental housing (Sec. 236).[28] Matusow complains because only a minority of the programs' funds went to poor families; he complains because some of the implementation of the programs evidenced corruption; and he complains because the programs created unwanted and unneeded new construction at the expense of the abandonment of existing properties.[29]

Matusow's first complaint, that the programs benefited those other than the poor, is a hollow one. He would have the reader believe that the fact that nonpoor are receiving benefits indicates that the program failed to work properly or that some corruption or inefficiency led to this state of affairs. The fact is that the programs were originally designed to benefit many nonpoor, so the fact that this occurred is not surprising or any indication of program failure or weakness.

Matusow's overproduction critique is equally weak. While it is true that a few cities may have large numbers of abandoned properties, it is gross oversimplification to charge that federal housing programs caused this phenomenon or that this housing was adequate or available to the poor. Many factors affect a landlord's decision to abandon property, and while unavailability of poor renters is one, other more important factors include the economic decisions of the landlord, the inability of poor renters to pay profitable rents, and general population shifts in central city areas:

In all, we lose perhaps 240,000 inner-city low-income units each year. Much of this loss is avoidable. In large measure, it represents tax advantages to the landlord for a finite period, with this incentive reinforced by increasingly impoverished tenants and the rent they pay. At some point it is profitable to disinvest and, ultimately, to abandon a no longer salvageable structure. In some measure also, housing loss represents a thinning out of center-city population, so that a higher income market does not claim these units.[30]

The poor still exist, and still need housing, even if they move from the center-city location where the landlord's marginal housing is located. And the fact that available units may exist there, or in other cities where the poor population is not now located and cannot now find jobs, does not help the poor find housing where they are now. Units available in St. Louis inner-city areas cannot help the Dallas poor find housing. Matusow ignores this important distribution and availability question.

The fact is that, like his colleague Charles Murray, Matusow never gets beyond the aggregate or past his examples to present to the reader an actual picture of the status of the poor during this period. It is interesting to know the number of housing units in St. Louis that have been abandoned and the fact that several corrupt officials in a few cities certified less than quality housing for program eligibility; but these historical examples tell us little about overall program accomplishments or about the actual impact housing programs are having on the poor and near-poor individuals who lived in substandard housing before the implementation of these programs (setting aside for the moment the significant number of nonpoor served by these programs).

Housing assistance programs, like private enterprises, come in almost infinite variations. They are not, as Matusow would have us believe, homogeneous. They differ in size, local conditions, degree of local and state government involvement, and clientele. And, like equally varied private-housing enterprises, some are more successful than others. What is amazing, and what Matusow does not tell you, is that so many public-housing efforts have served so many, so well, for so long—even the 1968 Housing Act. As Alvin Schorr points out, "the programs embodied in the Housing Act of 1968 . . . produced a two-thirds increase in the number of new housing units per year between 1970 and 1973. . . . Effects on family living have been impressive. In 1960, one household in eight lacked complete plumbing facilities; by 1980 that proportion was down to one in forty. In 1950, the average household had 1.5 rooms per person; it now has 2 rooms per person, and the rooms are larger."[31]

Additional figures on changes in the quality and quantity of housing from 1970 to 1979 point out even greater gains. Examining housing inadequacy in central cities from 1970 to 1979, Sternlieb and Hughes report a 76.4 percent reduction in the number of owner-occupied housing units missing plumbing facilities and a 48.6 percent reduction in rental units missing such facilities.[32] Clearly, the quality of housing units occupied by the poor improved significantly in this period.

In his critique, Matusow spends little time on the major poverty-housing program of the period—public housing. This federal, state, and local partnership program provides housing for over one million poor Americans. Most think of public housing as huge, high-rise projects in central cities, full of crime and decay and destined to be abandoned and torn down. The key example of this type of project is Pruitt-Igoe in St. Louis. Conservatives will point to this project as proof of the unworkability and failure of public housing. This is not the condition or fate of the typical public-housing project, however:

> Only 10 percent of all units are in large, high-rise projects. Extensive waiting lists testify that poor people regard public housing as superior to anything otherwise available to them. . . . "The social and physical problems among public housing projects vary considerably. Some projects are in good condition with few or no significant problems; others must be considered troubled because of their general condition and/or management problems. . . . A 1979 HUD study found that 67% of all housing projects were untroubled, with another 26% relatively untroubled."[33]

The key is one's expectations. Conservatives will be upset because 7 percent of public-housing projects can be classified as troubled. Others will be pleased because 90 percent have worked relatively well and because over a million unserved or underserved poor families are better housed than they otherwise would be.

Preschool Education

In the post–1965 period, the national government made a commitment to improve the relatively poor scholastic performance of many of the children of the poor. Recognizing the difficult family, neighborhood, and school environments many of these children faced, the basic idea was to provide a preschool experience that might enable the children to overcome these significant environmental difficulties. The program, initiated by the Office of Economic Opportunity, was called Head Start, and it contained five components: health, education, parental involvement, nutrition, and social and psychological services.[34] Unlike many of the other social-welfare programs, Head Start, while only modestly funded, around $350–400 million per year from 1967 to 1975,[35] was directed solely at the poor.

In spite of the fact that this is one of the only programs of this period whose clientele group consisted only of the poor, Charles Murray did not address the issue of Head Start. And in his 500-page book attacking the War on Poverty, Allen Matusow devotes little attention to the Head Start program. In commenting on it, Matusow does little more than grudgingly admit that "though falling short of early expectations, Head Start was nonetheless one Great Society program that worked."[36]

The fact is that, early expectations notwithstanding, the Head Start program was a case study in a successful poverty program. It was well focused, its goals were clear, and with very limited resources it achieved remarkable success in reaching its goals of improving the educational and social performance of poor children. Many of the program's major difficulties were not program-content related, but rather were political in nature and concerned certainty and level of funding and community political opposition.

The Head Start program is one of the most studied social-welfare programs. Longitudinal studies consistently show key and intended improvements in performance of Head Start participants over control groups. The major published works on Head Start—Zigler and Valentine's *Project Head Start* and The Consortium for Longitudinal Studies' *As The Twig Is Bent,*[37] systematically report the observable and significant positive impacts of this program. Head Start participants do significantly better than nonparticipating control groups on measures of health, achievement tests, achievement orientations, grade retention, and school completion.[38]

One study cited in these evaluations, whose findings are typical, is the Perry Preschool Project in Ypsilanti, Michigan. Following a group of preschool children since 1962, the researchers found that 22 years later, in 1984, their Head Start group had more employed, more high-school graduates, more college attenders, fewer arrests, fewer on welfare, and fewer teenage pregnancies than did nonparticipating control children.[39] Here we see a targeted poverty program that has in many respects succeeded in reaching its goals, yet its achievements are virtually ignored by the conservative critics of the post–1965 period.

Job Training

In the 1965–72 period, two major institutional job-training programs were implemented by the federal government—one as part of the Manpower Development Training Act (MDTA), a nonresidency institutional job-training program, and Job Corps, a residency-based program. These programs later evolved into the Comprehensive Employment Training Act program (CETA) and eventually into today's Job Training Partnership Act (JTPA). Like Head Start, the Job Corps Program and MDTA's institutional training were primarily targeted at the poor, and levels of funding were relatively less than those for more general social-welfare programs: In the 1965–72 period, Job Corps appropriations ranged from a low of $99 million in 1967 to a high of $318 million in 1968, while MDTA institutional ranged from $134 million in 1967 to $406 million in 1972.[40]

Both Murray and Matusow address the job-training issue and neither finds very much to argue for in these programs. In a way, both Murray and Matusow damn the job-training programs with faint praise. Both must, grudgingly, admit that the programs seemed to improve the status of those who took training, but both are quick to point out real or imagined shortcomings. Matusow, for example, in looking at Job Corps, says that "while many no doubt benefited from the experience, only a minority emerged notably more employable than before they began," and he highlights the program's relatively high drop-out rates, relatively unflattering comparisons to program no-shows, and the limited nature of the training.[41]

Murray's position is similar to Matusow's. "The programs were seldom disasters; they simply failed to help many people get and hold jobs that they would not have gotten and held anyway."[42] Murray then cites, and largely dismisses, the results of several studies showing income increases directly attributable to the training experience. The results are not high enough for Murray, who concludes, "Effects of this magnitude were far from the results that had been anticipated when the programs began."[43]

Matusow focuses on the Job Corps Program, and even though his book was published in 1984, you would think no analysis of Job Corps trainees occurred after 1967, the very first years of the program, for here are the main citations he refers to in his critique of the program. He does take general information about the nature of the program from a 1975 study by Levitan and Johnston,[44] which he cites as *The Job Corps*. However, as the full title, *The Job Corps: A Social Experiment that Works*, indicates, Levitan and Johnston's evaluation of the Job Corps Program is quite favorable, and they find much to laud in the effort. Although unreported by Matusow, Levitan and Johnston find important educational gains, job-placement gains, and wage gains.[45] They are careful to point out, however, the limitations of their analysis. Problems of self-selection to training and comparisons to no-shows reported in the 1967 Harris study[46] made it difficult to sort out the actual effects of the program itself in these early studies.

A more recent and comprehensive study of Job Corps effectiveness, however, which goes far beyond the initial two years emphasized by Matusow, published by Mallar, Kerachsky, and Thornton in 1980, and uncited by Matusow concludes that:

Job Corps is successful in achieving most of the desired impacts during the short-term post-program period. The desired impacts are particularly evident for Corpsmembers who complete the program, which appears to be at least in part attributable to program completion and not just to the underlying characteristics of completers. We also find that the beneficial impacts are not deteriorating as rapidly as had been previously suspected, and, in fact, employment and earnings impacts increase rapidly during the first three months that the Corpsmembers are out of the program after some initial problems for Corpsmembers when they reenter the labor market upon terminating from Job Corps.[47]

And Mallar, Kerachsky, and Thornton raise another important point—that benefits are not just limited to earnings and employment; they extend to other areas that help not only Corpsmembers, but the larger society as well:

The pattern of the averages for all Corpsmembers follows that for program completers—increased employment and earnings (after the immediate postprogram period), increased military service, increased education and training (except for high school), increased mobility (extremely large effects), reductions in health problems, reductions in welfare assistance, reductions in other transfers, reductions in drug and alcohol abuse, and reductions in criminal behavior.[48]

And, although their emphasis is on the short-term postprogram period, Mallar did hint that the benefits may be much more long-lasting: "Beyond the generally positive results, the most noteworthy finding is that these results appear to persist to the end of the seven-month observation period. In fact, if there is any trend after the first few months of postprogram experience, it appears to be toward increased program benefits. This pattern bears further examination, particularly with a longer observation period."[49]

Murray's critique is similar to Matusow's. While there may be some gains through job training, they are largely insufficient to merit the investment in the program. The problem again is one of expectation and subjective evaluation. Focusing on evaluations of the Manpower Development Training Act, Murray denigrates the gains reported. He emphasizes the results from two studies, one by Nicholas Kiefer and one by Orley Ashenfelter.[50]

Murray tells us that Kiefer, in his longitudinal study, finds only a 1.5 percent increase in wages that can be attributed to the training experience.[51] This is hardly anything to get very impressed about, Murray warns us. Let us look more carefully at what Kiefer was actually trying to do in his study. He was concerned about the problems of cross-sectional analysis in evaluating programs like MDTA. He felt that cross-sectional analysis artificially underestimated the actual accomplishments of the programs, and sought to test this proposition by looking at a longitudinal sample of program participants and a nonparticipant control group. The key point Kiefer was trying to make was a methodological one, that longitudinal analysis would give a more accurate and more positive evaluation of the effect of the training. For Kiefer, his effort was successful. He demonstrated that, contrary to cross-sectional studies finding diminished wages associated with training, his more appropriate methodology found the "true," positive program impact. Kiefer was much less concerned with the magnitude of the difference between the trainees and nontrainee control group, 1.5 percent, than is Murray. For Murray, it is the absolute difference reported by Kiefer that is important, and for Murray, it is too low.

This may be so, but remember, in his design Kiefer was essentially trying to make a methodological point about the preference of using longitudinal data for such comparisons. Therefore, when he constructed his control group, while he tried to match with the trainees as closely as possible, a perfect match was not possible. In fact, Kiefer's control group was substantially older than was the group of trainees—the mean age of the trainees was only 23.5 years, while for the nontrainee control group it was 27.4. This difference was not important to Kiefer, because it biased the findings against his hypothesis of finding greater positive earnings in the training group. Why is this so? Because we and Kiefer know that older persons develop more skills, have more job experiences, more time to advance in jobs, and so on than do younger workers. So Kiefer made the test harder on himself by having an older control group. The fact that he still found a 1.5 percent increase in earning for his younger group merely made his point more clearly.

For us, however, and for Murray, the 1.5 percent figure has other significance. Can it, as Murray would like us to believe, reflect the true gain for trainees over nontrainees? No, because the comparison group ages are too disparate and negatively biased against the trainee group. The important fact for us to notice is that even with the age factor against them, the trainee group still managed a 1.5 percent increase over the controls. This is a much stronger indication of the positive merits of the program than Murray would have us believe.

For Murray's reference to the Ashenfelter study, the problem is more one of subjective interpretation of the findings, rather than mistakes or omissions in their presentation. Once again we are looking at the glass half-full of water. Some may be terribly disappointed because it is half-empty while others may be excited and encouraged because it is half-full. In observing the same figures that Murray does, a $150–500 increase for males and a $300–600 increase for females in the immediate posttraining period, and some reduction five years later for males but not for females, one can come to a much more positive conclusion than does Murray about the worth of the program. In fact, Ashenfelter himself appears to do so. In making a comparison of the costs of the program to the benefits, he reports that his findings suggest that benefits meet program costs for males and are exceeded for females.[52] And his analysis of the benefits includes none of the indirect benefits in the areas of crime, welfare, military service, and so forth found to be present for Job Corpsmembers and almost certainly present for MDTA trainees as well.

Aid to Families with Dependent Children

Perhaps the most emotional and controversial area of post–1965 social policy is the Aid to Families with Dependent Children Program. It is a substantial program, several billions of dollars in state and federal outlays, and it is aimed directly at the very poor. For most Americans, recipients of this program's benefits are those one generally equates with the term "welfare recipient." Born out of the depression of the 1930s, this program was initially designed to help the children of poor families, usually headed by widows.[53] The expansion of the program over the years to include unwed mothers and the growth in dollar volume and minority clients have added to the public discontent with the program that has always been there.[54]

Charles Murray represents the basic conservative position on this most basic welfare program. The argument is simple and critical—welfare encourages dependency, and welfare subsidies increase rather than decrease poverty. It is interesting that conservatives persist in this set of beliefs, even after decades of empirical observation of the dynamics of the welfare rolls generally indicate that this fear is unwarranted:

The fear that individuals will prefer living off the public dole rather than earning their own way in society is a concern that is nearly as old as public assistance itself. . . . As a general characterization of AFDC caseload dynamics this scenario is clearly false. . . . Of all those who ever receive AFDC benefits, only a minority become long-term clients. Indeed, 50% of all AFDC episodes last less than two years. . . . recent studies have found that growing up in a welfare household does increase the likelihood of receiving welfare as an adult by a factor of 1.4 to 2. In absolute terms, however, the data also indicate that most children from welfare families do not grow up to receive welfare as adults.[55]

In view of these rather compelling statistics, Murray is forced to take another approach to demonstrate the merits of the conservative position. Consider, he says, the following hypothetical example—a couple, Harold and his pregnant girlfriend Phyllis, living in Pennsylvania. A close examination of the program benefits offered to them after 1960 and the implementation of all these welfare programs show a clear, rational bias in favor of their not working and not getting married. Before the implementation of these programs, Murray asserts, all the incentives would have been for Harold to seek minimum-wage employment and for them to get married. Here is proof positive, Murray tells us, of the insidiousness of the welfare programs, actually encouraging the very negative behaviors they are supposed to prevent.

There are two fundamental problems with Murray's hypothetical case against the poverty programs like AFDC. The first is that the benefit figures he uses to construct the choices available to Harold and Phyllis are neither representative, accurate, nor up to date. The second is that he never links his hypothetical-choice dilemma to any real events, real choices, or real behavioral actions of actual poor people. In other words, he never validates the appropriateness of his example to real-world poverty phenomena.

The appropriateness of the relative monetary advantages and disadvantages Murray presents for Phyllis and Harold have been directly and devastatingly challenged by Robert Greenstein. He argues that the key problems with Murray's case are that he presents the welfare benefits from one of the highest-paying welfare states, Pennsylvania, that he ignores benefits that can be received even while working or married, and that he stops his analysis in 1970, rather than carrying on to 1980, when the comparisons became even more favorable to working. Here is Greenstein's position in his own words:

> The Harold and Phyllis example is at the heart of Murray's case and is critical to the entire book. It is also flatly wrong. First, Murray's family budgets for 1960 and 1970 are not based on welfare benefit levels in an average state. Instead, his data is for the state of Pennsylvania. . . . Welfare benefits grew twice as fast in Pennsylvania from 1960 to 1970 as the nation as a whole. This allows Murray to portray the rise in ''incentives'' over the decade as being twice as large as they actually were. Murray makes a second error. In calculating the family's budget if Harold works, Murray incorrectly assumes Phyllis and her child cannot obtain food stamps. . . . The error makes working, compared to welfare, appear less attractive than it actually was.
>
> When the welfare vs. work comparisons are computed accurately, they show that taking a minimum-wage job was more profitable than going on welfare in most parts of the country in 1970. In some states with low welfare payments, such as southern states, minimum-wage jobs paid almost twice as much. . . . Murray's argument loses even more force when it's applied to the years after 1970. Although his book is subtitled *American Social Policy 1950–1980,* he never provides a 1980 family budget for Harold and Phyllis. If he had, he would have undermined his case. From 1970 to 1980, the incentives shifted strongly away from welfare and toward work.[56]

The second major problem with Murray's argument is that he presents no real data showing actual dependency behaviors or linking rates of benefits to increases in poverty or other negative behaviors like illegitimacy. For his example to be meaningful, he has to show us that these hypothesized choices actually are made by the poor and result in the negative behaviors he and the conservatives fear. We are told nothing by Murray about the representativeness of this example or if the hypothetical situations he describes represent actual events occurring in the real population.

Such a test is really quite simple. The variation in welfare (AFDC) benefits across the states provides an excellent laboratory within which to test Murray's hypothesis. If Murray is right, if people are enticed to poverty and dependency and other negative behaviors by attractive welfare benefits, then those states with higher benefit levels, those with the greatest enticements, should produce more of these negative behaviors. Figure 6.1 relates level of state AFDC payments to levels of state poverty and illegitimacy. On AFDC payments, states and the District of Columbia were ranked from 1 to 51, with 1 being the highest AFDC payment (Alaska) and 51 being the lowest (Mississippi). On percent below poverty, states and the District of Columbia were ranked from 1, highest poverty rate (Mississippi) to 51, lowest poverty rate (Wyoming). States and the District of Columbia were ranked on illegitimacy rate from 1 (highest—Mississippi) to 51 (lowest—New Hampshire).[57] If Murray and the conservatives are correct, then the inducements in the higher-benefit states should be encouraging higher levels of poverty and illegitimacy. The strongly negative correlation coefficients associated with the figure indicate just the opposite, however. Those states with the higher levels of AFDC benefits have lower, not higher, rankings on the negative behaviors Murray claims such benefits induce.

Even though Murray's assertion is clearly unsupported by the data, common sense will tell us that, overall, it is the general economic level of a state that most strongly correlates to poverty status. To be absolutely sure, therefore, that increases in AFDC payments were not encouraging marginal increases in state poverty levels, we need to recompute the correlations controlling for level of wealth within a state.[58] And when we do this, we find no change in the original relationships. The relationships between AFDC payment rank and poverty and illegitimacy, controlling for state wealth level, remain strongly negative ($-.42$ for poverty and $-.59$ for illegitimacy.)[59] Without question, levels of state AFDC payments are having no impact on poverty "seeking" among the marginal poor. Quite the contrary, higher state AFDC spending is associated with improvements in poverty and illegitimacy. According to these figures, spending more appears to help the poor, not hurt them.

Even if Murray correctly presented the alternative choices available to poor families like Harold and Phyllis, which he does not, for most social scientists it is neither surprising nor unusual that the relationships posited by Murray do not hold when tested empirically. Conservatives like Murray, in assuming the direction of the choice likely by Phyllis and Harold, assume one, very simplistic explanation of human behavior—the search for greatest economic gain. While it is true that this is an important force in human behavior, it is neither the only nor the most important in many behaviors. It is really likely that one makes decisions about work, marriage, and pregnancy solely for what these actions will bring in personal economic return? Psychologists and sociologists who have studied such behaviors for decades know that these behaviors arise from very complex considerations of personal psychological and external environmental factors, where considerations of personal economic gain play only a part. Personal identity, the need for individual achievement, intrinsic motivations, and external social pressures and structures are all important factors affecting decisions about work, marriage, and parenthood.[60]

Figure 6.1
Correlation between State AFDC Payments and State Poverty and Illegitimacy Rates

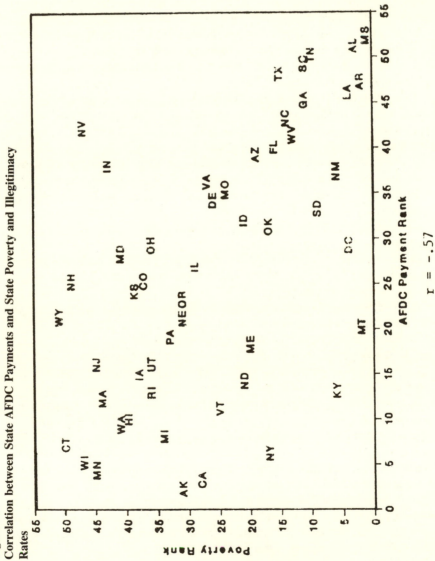

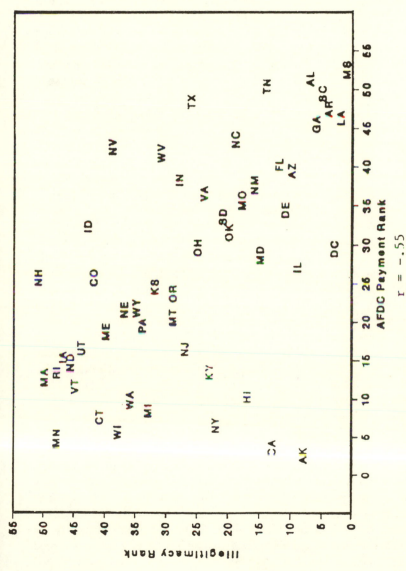

AFDC Payment Rank

$r = -.55$

Illegitimacy Rank

Source: Constructed by the author. Data on AFDC monthly family payments and on percent below poverty are from U.S. Department of Commerce, Bureau of the Census, *Statistical Abstract of the United States, 1987* (Washington, DC: U.S. Government Printing Office, 1987), pp. 365, 442; illegitimacy rate data are from U.S. Department of Health and Human Services, Public Health Service, National Health Care Statistics, *Vital and Health Statistics: Birth and Fertility Rates for States*, Series 21, No. 42, Washington, DC, 1980.

CONCLUSION

Conservatives, moderates, and liberals can legitimately disagree on the degree to which government is obligated to assist less fortunate citizens and the morality or justice inherent in taking resources from some citizens to assist others. When this argument leaves these value questions, however, and proponents or opponents use empirical observations of the effects of programs to make their point, they must be ready to defend their assertions, observations, and interpretations against tough empirical scrutiny. When the position of conservatives like Murray and Matusow on the failure of social programs is examined in such a way, it is found to be seriously flawed. In the areas of health, job training, AFDC, preschool education, and housing that we examined in some detail, systematic evaluation of the conservative assertions of failure are found to be the result of selective data presentation, reasoning by example without empirical validation, or selective and incorrect reading and reporting of the findings of published work.

The in-depth review of the programs presented here indicates that they were far from the abject failures Murray, Matusow, and their conservative allies would like us to believe. The conservatives exaggerate both the expectations and intentions of the programs and denigrate their accomplishments. Matusow, Murray, and the conservatives are upset because President Johnson declared war on poverty, a number of programs ensued, much money was spent, and yet poverty persists. This position is fundamentally a straw-man argument.

Contrary to the expectations about the War on Poverty, which Murray and Matusow seem so disappointed in and on which they base much of their criticism, presidential rhetoric does not equate to public policy. Policies are made after much debate and compromise by Congress and the president, by the House and the Senate, by Republican and Democratic legislators, and by conservative, moderate, and liberal lawmakers. The post–1965 programs were the result of real compromises by real politicians seeking diverse social and political ends. The reality of these programs is that they were never designed to end poverty, presidential rhetoric to the contrary. They always had many purposes, only one of which was to benefit the poor. That poverty was not ended, even though President Johnson declared war on poverty, does not indicate failure of the programs that ultimately were passed and implemented in his own and subsequent administrations. The programs must be judged on their own terms and for their own targets and funding levels.

At best, these programs were designed and funded at levels that enabled some poor to rise above the poverty line, to improve their quality of life (health, housing, and nutrition), and to enable some to be more employable and upwardly mobile. And within this limited effort, they were successes, not failures. The programs examined here, and others, like Social Security, have had major positive impacts. Social Security, for example, while not widely discussed by Murray or Matusow, has been a major force in reducing poverty among the aged in the United States. While it is an entitlement program, not a means-tested welfare one, the fact remains that Social Security has had a tremendous impact on reducing poverty among the aged. "One-third of the nation's poor families in 1962–32 million families—were headed by someone 65 years old or older. . . . Though 20 percent of all families were poor, nearly 50 percent of families with an elderly head were poor. Clearly poverty among the elderly was a serious problem."[61] By 1983 less than 15 percent of elderly families lived in poverty.[62] "Without their Social Security benefits, it is estimated that over half of the elderly would have incomes below the official poverty standard instead of the less than 15 percent that lived below the poverty line in 1983."[63]

The implicit argument in the conservatives' position is that more could have been accomplished for the poor by doing and spending less. Fewer programs spending less money would, according to conservative dogma, result in less dependence and less poverty. While the previous discussion has cast serious doubt on this position, we were in fact, during the Reagan years engaged in a social experiment that could test this proposition. In his administration President Reagan did what the conservatives argued for—spending less for programs targeted at the poor. In a number of welfare programs, especially AFDC, substantial cuts occurred in program benefits during the Reagan years. "The administration chose to change twenty-seven specific AFDC policies in such a way that fewer people would be eligible for benefits and many of those that were eligible would receive reduced benefits."[64] As a result of these specific AFDC policies, earnings of poor families dropped significantly and poverty rates increased. "The 1981 policy changes meant a complete loss of AFDC benefits for nearly half a million families. . . . Losing AFDC benefits meant less income and more poverty for these families," and as a result, poverty rates increased significantly in the states.[65]

It has not been only AFDC beneficiaries who have suffered under Reagan's social experiment. Gallup surveys comparing people's views of their economic position during the decade from 1974 to 1984 report increasingly bad times in 1984. In 1974, 14 percent of Americans said they did not have enough money for food, while by 1984, this number had risen to 20 percent; in 1974, 19 percent of those sampled by Gallup said they did not have enough money for clothes, but in 1984, this number had risen to 26 percent; in 1974, 15 percent of Americans said they did not have enough money for health care, while in 1984, this number had risen to 25 percent; and while 25 percent of citizens in 1974 reported worrying about family expenses, this number had grown to 35 percent in 1984.[66] Contrary to conservative expectations, spending less for the poor does not reduce the burdens of poverty; it increases them.

What, then, are people in the United States to do? It is clear that the conservative criticism of the social-welfare programs of the post–1965 period is largely without foundation, and it seems patently obvious that spending less will not accomplish more. Liberals and conservatives alike, however, will agree that the post–1965 social-welfare programs have not alleviated all poverty in the United States, nor could they. These programs have not necessarily focused on the poor, they have not always been funded at very high levels, and they have been intermittently and inconsistently supported politically. And while general improvements in the nation's economy will, as Ellwood and Summers point out, help many of the marginally poor, there remains a cadre of hard-core poor. These hard-core poor, because of previous poverty status, age, disability, limited skill level, or distrust of social, political, or economic institutions, born out of past discriminatory practices, may not benefit much from general improvements in the economy. For all of these reasons, a substantial number of U.S. citizens remain at risk to poverty and its consequences. What we do about this significant problem depends on our commitment to our fellow citizens and our level of understanding of the nature of poverty and the true merits and demerits of the programs available to us to remedy it. We cannot depend on ideological positions to provide us the knowledge base we will need to make these important decisions.

NOTES

1. President Reagan, State of the Union Address, February 4, 1986, reported in the *New York Times,* February 5, 1986, p. A20.

2. Charles Murray, *Losing Ground: American Social Policy 1950–1980* (New York: Basic Books, 1984).

3. Robert Greenstein, "Losing Faith in 'Losing Ground,' " *New Republic,* March 25, 1985, p. 14.

4. Murray, *Losing Ground,* p. 57.

5. Murray, *Losing Ground,* p. 58.

6. David T. Ellwood and Lawrence H. Summers, "Is Welfare Really the Problem?" *Public Interest* 83 (Spring 1986): 64.

7. Murray, *Losing Ground,* p. 64–65.

8. Murray, *Losing Ground,* p. 63.

9. Murray does not completely ignore the economic-system problem with his argument, but he tries to skirt it by simply asserting that the economy was better in the 1970s than the 1960s, and to prove his point he compares the two average GNP scores for each decade. This terribly oversimplified indicator misses all the ups and downs of the economy in both periods, but especially masks significant problems in specific years of the 1970s, which will be pointed out later.

10. Ellwood and Summers, "Is Welfare the Problem?", p. 60.

11. U.S. Department of Commerce, Bureau of the Census, *Statistical Abstract of the United States, 1986* (Washington, D.C.: U.S. Government Printing Office, 1985), pp. 390, 432.

12. Department of Commerce, *Statistical Abstract,* p. 354.

13. Department of Commerce, *Statistical Abstract,* p. 354.

14. Department of Commerce, *Statistical Abstract,* p. 432.

15. Department of Commerce, *Statistical Abstract,* pp. 445, 450.

16. Department of Commerce, *Statistical Abstract,* p. 390.

17. Department of Commerce, *Statistical Abstract,* p. 97.

18. The Robert Wood Johnson Foundation, *Access to Health Care in the United States: Results of a 1986 Survey,* Special Report Number Two, 1987.

19. Robert Wood Johnson Foundation, *Access to Health Care*, p. 8.

20. Alvin L. Schorr, *Common Decency: Domestic Policies after Reagan* (New Haven: Yale University Press, 1986), p. 166.

21. Karen Davis, ''A Decade of Policy Developments in Providing Health Care for Low-Income Families,'' in *A Decade of Federal Antipoverty Programs: Achievements, Failures, and Lessons,* ed. Robert H. Haveman, (New York: Academic Press, 1977), p. 204.

22. Schorr, *Common Decency*, p. 167.

23. Davis, ''Decade of Developments,'' pp. 224–25.

24. Davis, ''Decade of Developments,'' p. 202; see, also, Michael Morris and John B. Williamson, *Poverty and Public Policy: An Analysis of Federal Intervention Efforts* (New York: Greenwood Press, 1986, p. 104, for an update of these figures. They report AFDC recipients as representing 66 percent of beneficiaries in 1985, but only 26 percent of the expenditures—72 percent of the expenditures went for disabled or elderly.

25. Gary W. Copeland and Kenneth J. Meier, ''Gaining Ground: The Impact of Medicaid and WIC on Infant Mortality,'' *American Politics Quarterly* 15 (April 1987): 268.

26. Morris and Williamson, *Poverty and Public Policy*, p. 112.

27. Allen J. Matusow, *The Unraveling of America: A History of Liberalism in the 1960s* (New York: Harper & Row, 1984).

28. Phyllis A. Wallace, ''A Decade of Policy Developments in Equal Opportunities in Employment and Housing,'' in Haveman, *Federal Antipoverty Programs*, pp. 351–52.

29. Matusow, *Unraveling of America*, pp. 232–37.

30. Schorr, *Common Decency*, pp. 145–46.

31. Schorr, *Common Decency*, p. 116.

32. George Sternlieb and James W. Hughes, ''Housing the Poor in a Postshelter Society,'' *Annals of the American Academy of Political and Social Science* 465 (January 1983): 112.

33. Schorr, *Common Decency*, p. 144.

34. George B. Brain, ''Head Start, a Retrospective View: The Founders, Section Z: The Early Planners,'' in *Project Head Start: A Legacy of the War on Poverty,* Edward Zigler and Jeanette Valentine (New York: Free Press, 1979), p. 75.

35. Julius B. Richmond, Deborah J. Stipek, and Edward Zigler, ''A Decade of Head Start,'' in Zigler and Valentine, *Project Head Start,* p. 142.

36. Matusow, *Unraveling of America*, p. 266.

37. The Consortium for Longitudinal Studies, *As The Twig Is Bent . . . Lasting Effects of Preschool Programs* (Hillsdale, N.J.: Erlbaum, 1983).

38. Zigler and Valentine, *Project Head Start*, and Consortium, *As The Twig is Bent, passium.*

39. Findings summarized in Christopher Connell, ''Preschool Education Pays Dividends for Poor Children,'' Associated Press story published in *Bryan–College Station Eagle,* September 14, 1984, pp. 1 and 7A.

40. *Special Analyses: Budget of the U.S. Government* (Washington, DC: U.S. Government Printing Office, 1968), pp. 104–5; 1969, p. 102; 1970, p. 137; 1971, p. 135; 1972, p. 138; 1973, p. 140; and 1974, p. 123.

41. Matusow, *Unraveling of America*, pp. 238–39.

42. Murray, *Losing Ground*, p. 37.

43. Murray, *Losing Ground*, p. 38.

44. Sar A. Levitan and Benjamin H. Johnston, *The Job Corps: A Social Experiment That Works* (Baltimore, MD: Johns Hopkins University Press, 1975).

45. Levitan and Johnston, *Job Corps*, pp. 83–101.

46. The Harris Job Corps no-show study is listed in Levitan and Johnston, as Louis Harris and Associates, *A Study of Job Corps "No-shows": Accepted Applicants Who Did Not Go to a Training Center* (February 1967), printed in U.S. Congress, House Committee on Education and Labor, Hearings on Economic Opportunity Amendments of 1967, 90th Congress, 1st session.

47. Charles D. Mallar, Stuart H. Kerachsky, and Craig V. D. Thornton, "The Short-Term Economic Impact of the Job Corps Program," in *Evaluation Studies Review Annual*, ed. Ernest W. Stromsdorfer and George Farkas, Vol. 5 (Beverly Hills, CA: Sage, 1980), pp. 355–57.

48. Mallar et al., "Short-Term Impact," p. 357. See, also, David A. Long, Charles D. Mallar, and Craig V. D. Thornton, "Evaluating the Benefits and Costs of the Job Corps," *Journal of Policy Analysis and Management* 1 (Fall 1981): 55–76.

49. Mallar et al., "Short-Term Impact," p. 357.

50. Nicholas M. Kiefer, "Population Heterogeneity and Inference from Panel Data on the Effects of Vocational Education," *Journal of Political Economy* 87, (October 1979): s213–s226; and Orley Ashenfelter, "Estimating the Effects of Training Programs on Earnings" *Review of Economics and Statistics* 60 (February 1978): 47–57.

51. Murray, *Losing Ground*, p. 38.

52. Ashenfelter, "Effects of Training Programs," p. 316.

53. Morris and Williamson, *Poverty and Public Policy*, p. 54.

54. Morris and Williamson, *Poverty and Public Policy*, p. 54.

55. Morris and Williamson, *Poverty and Public Policy*, pp. 55–57.

56. Greenstein, "Losing Faith," pp. 12–13.

57. These figures were computed from data gathered by the author. AFDC monthly payments for a family, by state, are from the *Statistical Abstract of the United States, 1987*, p. 365. Illegitimacy rates are from *Vital and Health Statistics: Birth and Fertility Rates for States*, U.S. Department of Health and Human Services, Public Health Service, National Health Care Statistics, Series 21, No. 42.

58. The income measure used is personal income per capita, 1984, from U.S. Department of Commerce, *Statistical Abstract of the United States, 1986*, p. 440.

59. Similar zero-order and partial correlation findings are reported by Ellwood and Summers, "Is Welfare the Problem?" pp. 70–71.

60. The literature on these topics in sociology and psychology is so voluminous that one could not begin to cite even a small portion of the relevant research here. For a few typical works, just in the area of work behavior, see Clayton P. Alderfer, *Existence, Relatedness, and Growth: Human Needs in Organizational Settings* (New York: Free Press, 1972); Victor H. Vroom, *Work and Motivation* (New York: Wiley, 1964); Edward E. Lawler, III, *Motivation in Work Organizations* (Monterey, CA: Brooks/Cole, 1973); and Edward E. Lawler, III, *Pay and Organizational Effectiveness: A Psychological View* (New York: McGraw-Hill, 1971).

61. Lawrence E. Lynn, Jr., "A Decade of Policy Developments in the Income-Maintenance System," in Haveman, *Decade of Antipoverty Programs*, p. 67.

62. Ellwood and Summers, "Is Welfare the Problem?" p. 59.

63. Tom Joe and Cheryl Rogers, *By The Few for The Few: The Reagan Welfare Legacy* (Lexington, MA: Lexington Books, 1985), p. 23.

64. Joe and Rogers, *By the Few,* p. 33.
65. Joe and Rogers, *By the Few,* pp. 98–99.
66. *The Gallup Report,* January/February 1984, Report Nos. 220/221, Princeton, NJ: The Gallup Poll, pp. 22–26.

7

Lessons from Abroad

Americans are currently in a period of reflection and critical self-examination of their economic accomplishments. For most of their lives, they have thought of themselves and their country as the strongest and most successful economic competitors in the world. They have ridden a crest of economic success that has been unmatched by any country in the world. High productivity, high profits, control of international markets, high employment, high standards of living, and technological leadership have been accepted as the norm for their nation's economic system.

Events of the last few years, however, have caused serious doubt about the origins and future duration of this supremacy. Increasing competition from abroad, loss of market share, growing trade deficits, and loss in the value of the dollar have shaken Americans' beliefs in their economic system. In the past few years we have seen a tremendous increase in the economic performance of nations that we once considered inferior to us in technological skill and entrepreneurial talent. We have been shown that we are not the sole possessors of economic wherewithal and that increased competition can limit our economic power.

In spite of years of success, policies that helped guide the nation's economy to great heights are now seen as problematic and short-sighted. The success of other economic systems, particularly the Japanese, has led us to question our policies and look for alternatives to help us regain our former economic greatness. The Japanese have evidenced significant economic success these past several years: low unemployment (seldom exceeding 2 percent), substantial trade surpluses (particularly vis-à-vis the United States), substantial economic growth (greater than 4 percent during most of the 1980s), and increased productivity of its work force (rates of growth in productivity exceeding those of most Western countries, including the United States). During times like these, when we feel we may not be doing as well as we should, or as well as we have done in the past, we are tempted to look at the real or perceived "greater" success of others, like Japan, and wonder; Have we been doing things wrong? Do they do them better? If we only did what they do, perhaps we could be as successful.

Americans of all political persuasions are wondering what we have done wrong and what lessons the success of foreign nations, like Japan, may hold for us. Each of us tends to look through his own ideological lenses to search for the principles to guide us back to economic preeminence. For U.S. conservatives, then, it is not surprising that the success of nations like Japan is seen as stemming from their greater adherence to conservative, free-market policies and programs. The policies they oppose in the United States as being anti-free-market in their orientation are seen as being less present in the policies of the most successful foreigners, particularly the Japanese.

George Gilder tells us our more successful foreign competitors have less government spending and lower taxes.[1] Milton Friedman tells us they have less government intervention in and planning of the economy. He is quick to explain late-nineteenth-century Japanese success by simply asserting that the Japanese adopted the policies of Adam Smith. Other more recent and less successful economic experiments, like India's, he tells us, result from abandoning Smith and embracing centralized economic planning.[2] President Reagan and members of his administration continually emphasized other, "nonconservative" policies, which they blamed for most of our economic problems—high deficits, high inflation, and lack of saving.

The position of many conservatives is that the greater success of foreign nations is derived from their adhering to conservative principles. This position is summarized clearly in an article published in the conservative *Cato Journal*. Speaking of the success of Japan, the author asks rhetorically, "How then did Japan accomplish its phenomenally high economic growth rate after World War II? The 'secret' of Japan's growth can be stated in the simplest terms—a basically free-market economy, functioning effectively with minimal government intervention since the war."[3]

Are these depictions of the success of our competition and the weaknesses in us correct and complete? Have the Japanese embraced the free-market principles of Adam Smith, and is this the reason for their success? Are they really that successful? What, if any, are the lessons we can learn from the Japanese that might be useful in facilitating economic growth in the United States? These are complicated questions. And as might be expected, the answers are much more complex and less free-market-based than conservative rhetoric would have us believe.

Conservatives need and want to see in others' successes the application of their own ideological principles. If Japan is so successful economically, and to conservatives it clearly is, surely it must be because they embrace and apply conservative, free-market principles. The conservative spokesman in the *Cato Journal* tells us that lower taxes, lower welfare, greater individual entrepreneurship, less social security, small and balanced budgets, and less government intervention—all important conservative principles—explain the Japanese success.[4] As we shall see, however, these assertions are a gross oversimplification of the political, economic, and cultural realities that underlie Japan's economic "miracle." In the following pages we will examine the actual policies and accomplishments of the Japanese and compare them to those in the United States and other countries.

WORK, PRODUCTIVITY, SOCIAL WELFARE, AND THE CULTURE OF INDEPENDENCE

Listening to the conservatives, one gets the impression that Japanese citizens are harder-working, more productive, more independent, and more frugal than are their U.S. counterparts. Here, in the Japanese, the conservatives feel they have found the superior culture of success they find lacking in many Americans. Here is the rugged individualistic, independent, meritocratic, success-oriented culture that, for conservatives, drives the free-market machine to perfection and progress.

The Japenese would be very surprised to see themselves characterized in this way. They are a much more group-oriented, public-serving culture than the individualistic ideal assigned by the conservatives.[5] A long-time student of Japanese culture, Ezra Vogel, has emphasized this important characteristic of the Japanese: "The Japanese have been on the forefront of making large organizations something people enjoy. Americans tend to think of the organization as an imposition, as an outside force restraining the free individual. Japanese from an early age are taught the values of group life."[6] The Japanese are not the rugged, free-market individualists the conservatives portray them to be. Japan's culture is much more a hierarchical, group-oriented culture, where families, firms, and other collectivities play an important controlling and directing role, and from which individuals receive much of their identity and sense of accomplishment.

This is not to say, however, that the Japanese are not hard-working and productive. They are. They work more hours per year than either Americans or most Western Europeans. "Japanese workers still spend about 2,100 hours a year on the job—roughly 300 hours more than American workers and between 400 and 500 more than western Europeans."[7] And this increased work activity has resulted in gains in productivity. These increases in productivity, however, must be placed in proper perspective.

Japan's tremendous success in productivity growth does not mean that U.S. workers have been or are unproductive by comparison. Sociologist Jon Alston, a student of the Japanese experience, has stressed this:

Americans, and foreigners in general, forget that the United States economy has a higher overall productivity level than any other country, even Japan. The United States enjoys, or earns, the highest level of real gross domestic product (RGDP) per employed person of any industrialized nation in the world. This RGDP index measures the average output of all employed persons. Using the United States' output as an index of 100, the United States is close to ten percent more productive than its nearest rivals, Canada, France, and Germany. Japan is a poor fourth.[8]

Alston does caution, however, that Japanese productivity growth is rising rapidly and is likely to overtake us. He is particularly concerned about Japan's significantly greater increase in productivity in the manufacturing sector: "The annual manufacturing productivity increase during the period 1960–1981 for the United States was 2.7 percent; for Japan the same annual rate of increase was 9.2 percent."[9]

Japan's productivity accomplishments in the manufacturing sector are not, however, matched in other aspects of their economy. As Jon Woronoff argues,

What has been accomplished in manufacturing has not been reproduced, or even attempted, in other sectors. . . . in the secondary sector, utilities and especially construction have done very poorly, showing a minimal or negative growth. In the tertiary sector, most branches are relatively low, the weakest being services. . . . This also shows Japan in a much less flattering light as compared to other countries. True, manufacturing productivity has risen strikingly. But not the rest. Thus Professor Kazukiyo Kurosawa of the Tokyo Institute of Technology, one of the very few experts on non-industrial productivity, still rated America's overall performance considerably better for 1978 (on a scale of Japan's performance = 100), a good 160 to Japan's 100. That was because, although manufacturing productivity was only 115 (for America), agriculture and distribution plus services were much higher in the United States at 277 and 156 to Japan's 100. He recently evaluated the productivity of American white-collar workers at 130–150 against Japan's 100.[10]

With the percentage of the nonmanufacturing portion of the work force growing in both countries, the U.S. edge in nonmanufacturing productivity coupled with modest productivity increases in its manufacturing indicate that it is unlikely that it will continue to suffer a serious fall in productivity comparisons with Japan. This does not mean that Americans can be complacent about productivity, but it does indicate that they have much less to be ashamed about and much more to be proud of than conservatives seem willing to allow them.

This same caveat is true in the area of individual-citizen saving behavior. The conservatives are again partially right here. The Japanese do save a greater portion of their income than do Americans and Western Europeans. Table 7.1 presents gross saving as a percent of Gross Domestic Product (GDP) and net household saving as a percent of disposable household income for the United States, Japan, Germany, and the United Kingdom for available and representative years 1960–85.[11] From these figures it is clear that overall, and as individual households, Japanese are saving significantly more than others.

Table 7.1
**Gross and Household Saving Comparisons for the United States, Japan,
Germany, and the United Kingdom, 1960–1985**

Year	Nation			
	U.S.	Japan	Germany	U.K.
Gross Saving as a Percent of GDP				
1960	19.8	33.0	28.9	18.1
1975	18.1	32.3	20.9	15.5
1980	19.2	31.3	21.8	18.4
1985	16.5	31.7	22.2	19.2
Net Household Saving as a Percent of Disposable Household Income				
1960	7.2	17.4	8.6	4.5
1975	11.0	22.8	15.1	8.4
1980	9.1	17.9	12.8	11.0
1985	7.3	16.0	11.4	6.7

Source: Organization for Economic Cooperation and Development.   Historical
Statistics 1960–1985.   Paris, 1987, p. 70.

There are three important and unanswered questions about this savings phenomenon that must be addressed before we can evaluate its relevance to conservative assertions about superior Japanese cultural values and their relation to
free-market success: (1) Why is this savings rate so high? (2) How much saving
is really needed to support the capital formation associated with strong economic
growth? (3) What price have the Japanese had to pay in reduced consumption
and standard of living to support this high rate of saving?

Conservatives would have us believe that Japanese save more because reduced
government expenditures for social security make it imperative that individuals
save to be able to support themselves in their later years. ''Another important
motive for savings could well be the inadequacy of the government's social
security, welfare, and public housing programs. This inadequacy forces individuals and families in Japan to provide for their own security after retirement.''[12]
The inference conservatives want us to draw from this is clear. In the United
States we coddle our elderly with a Social Security blanket that relieves them
of the need to save for their own support. We could get more saving, then, if

Table 7.2
Social Security Transfers as a Percentage of GDP

Year	U.S.	Japan	Germany	U.K.
		Nation		
1960	5.0	3.8	12.0	6.8
1975	11.1	7.7	17.6	9.9
1980	10.9	10.1	16.5	11.5
1985	11.0	11.0	16.1	14.0 (1984)

Source: OECD *Historical Statistics 1960-1985*. Paris, 1987, p. 63.

we reduced this dole and forced our elderly to save in order to fend for themselves, as the Japanese have done. There are several flaws in this reasoning, however.

First, the Japanese social-security blanket is not very different from that provided in the United States. Table 7.2 presents social-security transfers as a percent of GDP for the United States, Japan, Germany and the United Kingdom for selected years, 1960–85. The figures show that since 1980, the Japanese have spent as large a proportion of their GDP on social-security transfers as has the United States. Both have spent substantially less than Germany, which we saw in Table 7.1 had the second-highest saving rate. High social-security payments in Germany do not, therefore, appear to be stifling savings. And similar rates of social-security transfers in Japan and the United States seem to indicate that they could not be the source of old-age fears in Japan, which conservatives argue are fueling their drive for savings. The argument that social-security fears lead to savings is further deflated when one remembers that similar GDP percentages spent on social-security transfers, in Japan and the United States reflect quite different proportions of elderly among their populations. In 1980 only 9 percent of Japan's population were aged 65 or above;[13] in 1980 the U.S. percentage was 11.3 percent.[14] So while as a percent of GDP, Japan and the United States have similar social-security transfers, on a per-person basis, the Japanese are receiving more of these transfers than are Americans. It seems very unlikely that old-age fears and lack of government coddling are the major source of saving behavior in Japan or, conversely, that government coddling and the lack of old-age fears are discouraging saving in the United States.

What, then, is at the root of the significantly greater saving behavior of the Japanese? The answer, conservatives will be sorry to learn, is government policy. The Japanese government has engaged in three specific sets of policies that have increased savings levels and reduced consumption levels among Japanese citizens. The first set of policies, which we will discuss in much greater detail later, has created various tariff and nontariff trade barriers that have resulted in very high consumer prices in Japan, for both domestically and foreign-produced products. Prices for major consumer goods in Japan are significantly higher than in the United States or European countries. Housing prices, land prices, utilities, durable goods, and food are 50–100 percent higher in Japan than in the United States.[15] People in Japan must save to be able to afford the very expensive large items they need.

The second and third government policies stimulating saving are closely related: low-interest, but relatively tax-free savings accounts, and relatively high-interest consumer loans. In 1980 interest rates on ordinary deposits at Japanese banks earned around 2.7 percent, while average loan rates were three times greater, 8.2 percent.[16] Because they want to buy high-cost items like homes and cars, and because they are discouraged by relatively high consumer-loan rates, Japanese are forced to save for large purchases. As Robert Samuelson has summarized the problem, "Interest rates on consumer deposits have long been held down by law. Paradoxically, this stimulated saving because consumers—earning less on their deposits—had to save more to meet their personal objectives: to buy a home, send children to college or enjoy retirement. Saving was also spurred by restricted consumer lending."[17] Government saving and lending interest-rate policies and the desire to purchase expensive items, not fear of falling through the social-security net, are the principal factors stimulating high savings rates in Japan.

Whatever their reason for saving, it is true that Japanese save more, and many, especially conservatives, feel this saving provided the capital growth needed to fuel Japan's economic growth. The implication is that low saving in the United States is, conversely, responsible for our lower levels of economic growth. It is clear that saving is needed for capital formation and economic investment. The question that must be addressed is the level of savings needed to provide needed capital formation and whether or not such savings need come from individuals, as the bulk of it does in Japan. Table 7.3 presents the GDP growth for our four comparison countries for selected years 1972–85, and Table 7.4 presents the gross fixed-capital formation data for the period 1960–85.

These two tables, taken with the savings reported in Table 7.1, tell an interesting story. First, changes in net household, that is, personal savings are not very strongly related to gross savings levels, savings from all sources, within countries. Gross savings are relatively stable over time, while net household-savings rates swing rather widely. Gross saving and gross fixed-capital formation track each other very closely, but changes in neither seem to be associated with within-country changes in GDP growth. And cross-country comparisons also present little support for a strong case that changes in saving and capital-formation rates are a principal factor in changes in GDP growth. Japan does have higher saving and capital-formation rates than the other three countries, and it does demonstrate consistently higher rates of GDP growth. Germany, however, has rates higher than those of the United States and the United Kingdom, but its

Table 7.3
Percentage Change in Real GDP, 1972–1985

	Nation			
Year	U.S.	Japan	Germany	U.K.
1972	5.1	8.4	4.2	2.3
1975	−1.0	2.6	−1.6	−0.6
1980	0.0	4.4	1.4	−2.3
1985	3.0	4.5	2.6	3.7

Source: OECD Historical Statistics 1960–1085, p. 44.

Table 7.4
Gross Fixed-Capital Formation as Percent of GDP, 1960–1985

	Nation			
Year	U.S.	Japan	Germany	U.K.
1960	18.0	29.5	24.3	16.4
1975	17.2	32.5	20.4	19.9
1980	19.1	31.6	22.7	18.2
1985	18.6	27.7	19.5	17.2

Source: OECD Historical Statistics 1960–1985, p. 65.

GDP growth from 1972 on is not as good as that of the United States and only slightly better than that of the United Kingdom.

It is clear that saving and capital formation are important to economic growth, but they are only one part of a much more complex economic picture. Is there a saving and capital-formation threshold relative to economic development? Is 15 or 20 or 25 percent enough? Does more above that really help? To imply that positive changes in saving and capital formation equate with economic growth is a seriously misleading oversimplification. Economic success has occurred quite frequently for those with relatively low rates of saving and capital formation; and high rates do not guarantee consistent, positive economic results. High savings rates may have helped Japan, but they seem less beneficial to Germany; and lower savings rates cannot be directly tied to economic-growth problems in the United States. The data indicate that it seems rather pointless to assign low savings rates as a major culprit in the curent U.S. economic difficulty.

Do we want to follow Japanese policies and force greater savings among our population? The answer is no, for two reasons. The first was made clear above: Increased savings rates alone seem, at best, only a small factor in positive economic growth. The second reason for rejecting a policy of forcing greater savings, in the way the Japanese did, is that Japanese consumers have suffered because of the policy. Raising prices and reducing consumption have held down the standard of living of Japanese people. In spite of general, system-level economic success, individual Japanese consumers suffer in comparison to their U.S. counterparts. High prices for homes, food, and durable goods, resulting from government saving and consumption policies, have produced crowded, uncomfortable living conditions, little leisure time, and long waits for major purchases.[18]

"Japanese living standards remain more than a fifth below ours. Its efficient global industries coexist with far less efficient service and retail sectors. Many Japanese still work 5 1/2 or 6 days a week. New American homes are a third larger than new Japanese homes.[19] And Japanese consumers are becoming more unhappy with this situation. Chisholm and Schaniel report that in spite of their general cultural value of consensus and dislike of confrontation, significantly large numbers of Japanese, in a recent public-opinion survey, report dissatisfaction with their lives.[20] Forced saving and concomitant reduced consumption, higher prices, and lower standard of living are not lessons we want to learn, even if we felt such saving would lead to greater economic growth in our country, which it appears unlikely to do.

TAXES, DEFICITS, AND INFLATION

Listening to conservatives extol the virtues of a balanced budget and revile deficits, inflation, and taxes, while at the same time holding up Japan as the model we should follow, leads us to expect that Japan is not guilty of our excesses in these areas. Surely, to be a model for conservatives, Japan must be a paragon of balanced budgets, low deficits, low inflation, and low taxes. This turns out not to be the case, however.

The facts are that Japan has achieved much of its remarkable economic growth while at the same time experiencing both substantial budget deficits and inflation. In the very high economic growth period between 1976 and 1982, Japan's budget deficit increased from 3.8 trillion yen to over 9 trillion yen, or from about 4 percent of GDP in 1976, roughly equal to the U.S. deficit, to over 6 percent of GDP in 1982, nearly twice the deficit proportion experienced in the United States.[21] Japan was hardly following the conservative principle of a balanced budget during a period of its profound economic growth.

And the same is true for inflation. The increase in the consumer price index for all items in Japan for the period 1972–85 stood at 4.5 percent in 1972, 11.8 percent in 1975, 8.0 percent in 1980, and 2.1 percent in 1985; this compares with 3.3, 9.1, 13.5, and 3.5 percent, respectively, for the same years for the United States; for Germany, the comparable figures are 5.5, 6.0, 5.5, and 2.2 percent.[22] During most of the past two decades the inflation rate in Japan has been equal to or greater than that experienced in the United States and Germany, Japan's two greatest economic rivals. It would not seem that high inflation rates in Japan had the substantially negative economic impacts conservative dogma forecasts they will.

On the issue of taxes, too, the expectations created by conservative rhetoric do not square well with the actual facts. Conservatives would have us believe that, compared with the United States, the tax burden in Japan is substantially lower. Comparing taxes across countries is an especially difficult task. Nations differ tremendously in what they call taxes, in the published tax rates, and in their actual tax efforts when one controls for loopholes, deductions, and other exceptions. The result is that different investigators often assert conflicting levels of taxation for the same countries during the same time periods. For example, Jon Woronoff writes that the combined tax and social-security contributions for Japan in 1981 and the United States in 1978 (total tax revenue as a percent of national income) were 34.3 and 37.7 percent, respectively.[23] Similar figures for the year 1983 are reported in the *Japan Economic Almanac* of 1986.[24] Charles McMillan, however, in *The Japanese Industrial System,* asserts that the real, comparative tax burden, taking into account special tax-expenditure measures, is 52.5 percent for Japan and 37.95 percent for the United States.[25] Allen Manvel, writing in *Tax Notes* in 1986, presents yet another set of figures. He reports that taxes, including social-security "taxes," as a percent of GDP for Japan and the United States in 1973 were 22.47 and 29.27 percent, respectively; by 1983 Manvel reports the figures at 27.7 percent for Japan, an increase of 23 percent from 1973, and 29.03 percent for the United States, a decrease of 1 percent.[26]

This is a confusing array of numbers. Whichever figures one chooses to use, however, the picture of Japan as a low-tax nation compared with the United States is difficult to support. The similarity in level of taxes between the two nations may, however, be further demonstrated in a set of figures that cuts through some of the confusion in looking at taxes alone. We can look at total government receipts for a nation—the total revenue the government receives in all forms, including taxes, fees, payments, licenses, and the complete array of devices governments use to acquire revenue. This measure also, by looking at the total receipts, has controlled for various deductions and loopholes that may differ substantially across nations.

Table 7.5 presents the government receipts as a percentage of GDP for Germany, Japan, and the United States for the period 1960–85. While U.S. government receipts are slightly larger than Japan's up to 1980, by 1985 the receipts are virtually identical. And both countries' receipts are substantially lower than Germany's, where higher tax levels have not seemed to retard its significant

Table 7.5

Government Receipts as a Percent of GDP for Japan and the United States, 1960–1985

	Nation		
Year	Japan	United States	Germany
1960	20.7	26.3	35.0
1975	24.0	28.8	42.7
1980	27.6	30.8	44.7
1985	31.2	31.1	45.4

Source: OECD, Historical Statistics, 1960–1985, p. 64.

economic accomplishments. The data simply do not support an assertion that government taxing levels in Japan are substantially lower than those in the United States or that different taxing levels are associated with variations in each nation's level of economic success.

Conservatives might respond to these findings by arguing that even though tax levels are relatively the same or only slightly higher in the United States, the Japanese may tax differently than we do. Perhaps, in deference to conservative wishes and hopes, the Japanese may tax corporations less or may have less progressive taxes than we do. It may be, then, that by following these conservative policy suggestions, the Japanese are more "helpful" even though overall tax levels are not as low as the conservatives would like them to be.

This does not seem to be the case, however. In their own country, Japanese place rather stiff tax burdens on their corporations. Large corporations in Japan pay about 55.5 percent of their net income in taxes, much more than do most corporations in the United States.[27] A rate this high in the United States is found only for corporations making $100 million dollars or more (less than 1 percent of all corporations in the United States); the average tax rate for the next largest group of U.S. corporations, asset size $10 million to $99.9 million, is less than 20 percent.[28] Corporations' share of total taxes in Japan in 1985 was over 30 percent, up from only 9.5 percent before World War II, while U.S. corporations' share of federal income taxes in 1985 was only 9 percent down from 17 percent in 1970.[29]

Not only are corporations relatively heavily taxed in Japan, but taxes there are also fairly progressive, even by U.S. standards. Rates for the highest earners in Japan are significantly higher than in the United States. Japanese taxpayers today who earn the equivalent of $80,000 a year have reached a marginal tax rate of 70 percent.[30] In the United States today, a person making $80,000 pays

at a marginal tax rate of 38.5 percent.[31] Conservatives cannot point to Japanese
tax levels or tax-distribution policies to find conservative explanations of Japanese
economic success.

THE ROLE OF GOVERNMENT INTERVENTION

If saving, productivity, independence, taxes, deficits, and inflation do not
explain the Japanese economic success, we must look elsewhere for those factors
that truly underlie Japan's successful economic progress. One important source
is not difficult to find, and it is one that conservatives will not like to have
discussed. It is the tremendous guidance, leadership, assistance, direction, and
protection provided Japanese business by the Japanese government.

It is, therefore, quite surprising to see conservatives, like those writing for
the *Cato Journal,* claim that Japanese economic success is the result of the
absence of government intervention in the economy. This is clearly a case of
wishful thinking and tunnel vision. Every major scholar of Japanese economic
development would find this conservative assertion incredible. Virtually every
serious student of Japanese economic progress stresses the significance of the
government policies that underlie Japan's rapid economic achievements. These
policies include government loans in support of specific industries, research and
development assistance, regulation, planning, building government and business
and business-business partnerships, targeting of industrial sectors, facilitating
licenses, supporting private loans and initiatives, and protection from foreign
competition. Compared to our experience in the United States, government
intervention in the Japanese economy has been massive and pervasive and its
impact on the Japanese economy profound.

One hardly knows where to begin in chronicling the interventions Japanese
government has utilized to assist and further the country's economic development. A good place to start is the myriad of government agencies, like the
Agency of Industrial Science and Technology, the Fair Trade Commission or
the best known, Ministry of International Trade and Industry (MITI), which uses
government frunds and influence to direct a substantial part of Japan's economic
activity. While these agencies, like MITI, may provide some direct loans to
targeted agencies, such government loans themselves may be the least important
weapon in their arsenal of control over Japanese business activities.

Through their integrated contacts with the private sector, these agencies set
the tone and direction for appropriate business activity and provide the signal
for other government agencies and the private sector to fall in line behind government policies. Through their power to grant licenses, patents, export credits,
and other needed support, as well as their control over some government funds
and their key influence over other public and private funds, these agencies exert
a tremendous influence over Japanese economic activity.[32] Vogel has summarized
the far-reaching impact of a particularly important agency, MITI.

MITI officials have power to grant licenses and patents and to determine which firms will participate in which projects, but the real power of MITI rests on the quality of its information, the care it takes in consulting with outsiders, the persuasiveness of its arguments, and the will to use its persuasiveness to favor those firms that cooperate. . . . Business leaders generally follow MITI's advice. They know that its officials are willing to exercise their authority when challenged and, more importantly, they know that MITI's advice represents more than bureaucrats' views; it represents the distillation of broad consultation. Companies know that MITI's advice, once formulated, has great influence with banks, politicians, other parts of the bureaucracy, and other industrial and commercial sectors as well, and they are rarely willing to challenge it.[33]

Through engaging in every activity from special tax benefits and deductions[34] to forcing small industries to merge to become more competitive with foreign competitors,[35] from making loans directly to encouraging private loans, from direct allocation and rationing resources to licensing and approval authority,[36] the Japanese government has become, in the words of Keniche Ohmae, the coach and cheerleader of the Japanese economic system.[37] And these are just some of the activities and powers of the formal, central government agencies, like MITI. Japan also has over 100 public policy companies, public corporations, which also control and direct much economic activity for the government. Chalmers Johnson has argued that the 112 public corporations in Japan control over 40 percent of the national budget and 5 percent of the nation's GDP.[38]

Up to now, we have been focusing only on the direct help and direction the Japanese government provides to its economic system. There is another, perhaps as important, indirect mechanism the government has used extensively to facilitate the economic development and competitiveness of its industries and businesses. This is the use of protectionist trade policies. Through the implementation of stiff tariff and nontariff barriers, the Japanese government has prevented significant foreign competition from penetrating Japanese home markets and weakening the position of indigenous industries.

The litany of protective devices used by Japanese officials to restrict foreign competition in their home market is well known to Americans. From semantic technicalities to direct quotas, from arbitrary and unnecessary "safety" inspections to less subtle restrictions on market entry and product distribution, the Japanese government has followed anything but a policy of free trade regarding the openness of its markets to foreign products. Ezra Vogel tells a story about kidney dialysis machines that is both typical and illustrative of the problems foreign products face in penetrating Japanese markets.

When a foreign kidney dialysis machine began to take over the market because it was able to do in several hours what it took Japanese-made machines fourteen hours to do, the Japanese health service changed its rules to pay for use of dialysis machines on the basis of length of time machines were used, so that Japanese health facilities again began to buy Japanese products, subjecting patients to fourteen hours of time for what could have been done in several hours.[39]

These kinds of protectionist policies, which have helped guard the market share and profitability of Japanese firms and which have bought them the time needed to improve their operations without the press of immediate foreign competition and income loss, are not the kinds of policies likely to be endorsed by conservative, free-market advocates in the United States.

THE LARGE SCALE OF BUSINESS IN JAPAN

As we saw in Chapter 5, conservatives, following the principles of Adam Smith, like to think successful national economies are the result of free-market competition provided by the activities of millions of small entrepreneurs. The conservative *Cato Journal* piece reiterates this assertion concerning the Japanese success. "Through the market process—hundreds of thousands of private entrepreneurs' individual decisions and energy—rather than by the government's calculated direction, Japan's industrial structure has shifted to high value-added manufacturing industries."[40] The implication is clear. Lots of relatively small, creative, individual entrepreneurs are the driving force behind the Japanese success. Again, however, the facts of Japanese economic life do not square very well with conservative rhetoric.

The fact is that Japan's economy is one of the most centralized and concentrated in the free world. A few huge corporations control most of the economic wealth and power and, working with government, direct most of the economic activity of the nation. There is very little room for and very little evidence of the importance of small-scale entrepreneurial activity in Japan. In 1963, when Japan was launching its major economic move, the 100 largest nonfinancial corporations in Japan controlled over 50 percent of all paid-in corporate capital in Japan.[41] Japan's nine huge trading companies, called *Sogo Shosha*, multifaceted, vertically and horizontally integrated megacompanies, control about 50 percent of Japan's total exports and imports, the very lifeblood of the country's economic system.[42]

Entrepreneurial activity takes place within the network of established large firms in Japan. Corporate bureaucracies identify potentially profitable areas and invest corporate resources in developing those areas for the company. New developments spin off from and remain closely tied to existing large firms. The conservative's ideal, the small, individual, entrepreneurial risk taker, who has an idea and borrows or risks his own resources in an independent attempt to crack a market and get rich, is not the principal way entrepreneurial activity and its resulting economic development is channeled in Japan.

THE LACK OF A DEFENSE BURDEN

For nations to progress economically, they need to be at the cutting edge of technological developments in order to take advantage of new products and new, more efficient manufacturing techniques.[43] To be in this position, nations need to invest significant financial and human resources in the development and commercialization of new ideas. The most important indicator of this activity is the extent of the resources nations invest in research and development related to economic-development activities.

Here a stark difference can be seen between Japan and the United States. The support of defense-related activities has placed a burden on economic development in the United States that is not present in the Japanese economy. It is not just that we spend more on defense than the Japanese, although the differences are significant. In 1980 less than 3 percent of Japan's government expenditures went for defense.[44] while in the United States we spent more than 20 percent of our national government expenditures on defense.[45] The different spending levels are illustrative, but it is in other, more subtle areas that the true defense impact on economic development in the United States can be seen.

The problem occurs when important research resources and intellectual manpower, which could be used to create product- and process-related economic advancement, are diverted to largely defense-oriented activities, with limited spin-off of economic benefits. We need a good defense, and it is not inappropriate for us to invest significant resources in it, but we are clearly making trade-offs when we make such investments. Conservative economist Herbert Stein, in defending greater defense spending, has made this point very clearly:

We don't have a civilian economy and a defense economy. We have one economy, which has to meet the needs of the society. Amaerica needs missiles and it needs toasters, and at the moment its need for more missiles is more urgent than its need for more toasters. If we divert scientists from toasters to missiles, and make the production of missiles more efficient, we are making the economy work better to serve our needs.[46]

Stein has stated the problem very well. We can choose between investing our scientific and technological resources in defense or in commercial-product development. We may disagree with him on how much of our resources need to go to defense, but the problem of trade-offs is inevitable. It is a choice, however, which the Japanese economy has not had to make. Because of a very small defense commitment, they can and do invest most of their scientific and technological fiscal and manpower resources on economic-product development. This fact, not some weakness in our cultural or economic system, is a major reason they have advanced manufacturing technology and product development faster than we have. In a sense, by doing their defense research for them, we have subsidized their nondefense technological advances, which, in turn, compete with us.

This differential investment in nondefense scientific and technological advancement is demonstrated in public and private research and development (R&D) expenditures made in Japan and the United States. In 1981 the United States and Japan were spending about the same proportions of the GDP on R&D, about 2.5 percent.[47] Remember, a substantial portion of the U.S. R&D is in defense-related activities. When one compares the non-defense-related R&D expenditures, however, the ones that really drive economic innovation and growth, the figures look quite different. In 1981 Japan's nondefense R&D spending stayed at 2.5 percent of GDP, but U.S. spending dropped to about 1.8 percent of GDP.[48] U.S. government R&D expenditures illustrate the problem. In 1985 the U.S. federal government spent around $50 billion on R&D, but almost 70 percent of it went to defense (and this does not even include research expenditures for defense-related research components like NASA).[49] Since R&D is essential to obtaining new knowledge, greater investment in R&D should lead to greater economically related scientific and technological discoveries and greater ability to commercialize these discoveries. Without a defense burden, Japan can do more with a lower overall R&D investment. Japan is freer than we are to invest its resources in activities that relate more directly to economic development. The result is that they have recently made more economically important technological advances than we have. There is no need for us to find deep, ideologically related weaknesses in ourselves or our economy, or for us to seek ideologically related superiority within the Japanese, to explain these differences. Noted history of technology professor Walter McDougall of the University of California at Berkeley has put the problem in its proper perspective: "We can't put money into military R&D to stimulate the economy; we do it to defend ourselves. Some military technology helps the civilian economy and some doesn't, but there's absolutely no way you can predict. If your goal is to stimulate the civilian economy, you ought to spend your R&D stimulating the civilian economy."[50]

REAL LESSONS FROM THE JAPANESE EXPERIENCE

The Japanese have accomplished much and have much to be proud of concerning their substantial economic progress since their defeat in World War II. U.S. conservatives, however, who hope to assign this success to the application of free-market principles are presenting a skewed and inaccurate picture of the actual Japanese experience. As the above discussion has illustrated, large business concentrations, government intervention, and ability to concentrate resources in non-defense-related activities are more important in explaining this sucess than ideologically based notions of independent culture, individually based free-market competition, or limited government.

Rather than being a free-market paradise where individual competition and lack of government interference have produced an economic miracle, Japan is a group-oriented, heavily government-guided and regulated, power-and wealth-concentrated system. There are lessons we can learn from the policies they have utilized to achieve their economic growth. Which ones we can and want to try still must be decided. Some suggest that we can copy little from the Japanese because our political and social culture is so different from theirs. According to Issac Shapiro, writing in the *Wall Street Journal*,

For better or for worse, America is historically and irrevocably a decentralized, heterogeneous, multi-racial, multi-religious society. Is it conceivable that Americans will ever want to pay the price of emulating the Japanese? Is it reasonable to envisage an American system of centralized, uniform education aimed at producing group-orientted, conformist, patriotic, hard-working and civilly-obedient Americans who stand ready to sacrifice individual goals and abandon their right-consciousness for the sake of social harmony and greater productivity?[51]

The answer to Shapiro's question is probably no, but cultural transformation is hardly necessary. Acting within our own traditions we can adapt certain policies, found useful by the Japanese, to our system. We can achieve greater government–business cooperation, encourage greater business-business cooperation, invest greater resources in nondefense R&D, and protect young, important industries from foreign competition without perverting our sense of self or our fundamental social and political values.

While we do want and would not endure the tremendous centralization of government economic planning found in Japan, we can certainly work to create more positive, less confrontational methods of cooperation between business and government in this country. Government agencies can find ways, within our political traditions, to target and stimulate economic areas with high potential. As we have already seen earlier in this book, this is precisely what we did at other times in our history, from canal and railroad building to development of airplanes and computers. We can do more, if we invest more resources in the activity and if we find ways to work with business to help plan and focus economic resources where they provide the greatest potential for economic growth. Such activities are not foreign to us; they are parts of our economic past that need to be rediscovered and revitalized.

We cannot and probably do not want the large concentration of business activity that exists in Japan, but company-to-company cooperation, fostered by government policy, is an idea worth pursuing to a greater degree than we do now. By sharing resources and information across company lines, the Japanese have been able to make breakthroughs and commercialize them more rapidly than have other countries where competition prevents the flow of such information. Several major U.S. computer companies, including Honeywell and Digital Equipment, recognized this problem and formed, in 1983, one of the first U.S. interfirm research cooperative ventures, the Microelectronics and Computer Technology Corporation (MCC). The goal of the new corporation is to pool research resources and information across company lines to maximize possibilities for breakthroughs and commercialization of new technologies. Business and government need to find ways to encourage more cooperation of this type and to make sure that short-term, individual company jealousies and competitive urges do not limit the substantial potential such joint ventures offer our firms in meeting concentrated opposition from foreign competitors.

We can act more forcefully to protect new U.S. industries from predatory foreign competition. The Japanese did not invent protectionism but they have carried it further than most other countries. We in the United States tried various forms of protective tariffs in the post-Civil War period and through the turn of the century. And while historians then and today still debate the merits of those policies, there is evidence that they did foster certain growing industries and clearly did not hinder the development of the U.S. economy.[52]

All of this is not to suggest that we replicate the extreme protectionist measures employed by the Japanese, but it seems to this author that we may, within our political traditions and without launching a trade war, act scrupulously to protect certain young industries with promise from some degree of competition during their formative years. While we still have uncertainty about whether protective tariffs were principally responsible for such new industry establishment in our earlier history, the Japanese have no such doubts about their extensive protectionist policies. They believe strongly in their protective measures and guard them tenaciously. Future historians may argue about how important these protectionist measures were to Japanese economic success, but those closest to them now, the Japanese, clearly have their own view.

One of the easiest things we can do, and one that is well within our traditional way of behaving, is to invest greater government resources in nondefense R&D. Either by reducing expenditures in other areas, or by raising new revenues, we can commit ourselves to a high level of investment in consumer, product-oriented research and development. The business of researchers is to research. They must, however, do research in areas where appropriate levels of funding are available. In the United States, for the past several years, that area has tended to be defense. And with President Reagan's Space Defense Initiative, the trend has even accelerated. We must provide research resources for scientists and engineers who are willing and able to do basic and applied research in consumer, product-oriented areas. As McDougall has made clear, if we want to stimulate the civilian economy, we have to invest in civilian research. This research does not have to come at the expense of important defense needs. It must, however, be viewed as a separate and important aspect of our economic national security to advance knowledge that has the potential for economic growth and development.

Conservatives have a serious dilemma before them. They like and respect the economic achievements of countries like Japan, but are ideologically opposed to the real, non-free-market policies that are required to achieve such success. It is clear that the kinds of policies suggested by the Japanese experience to help economic growth in the United States will require more, not less, government investment and activity in the economy.

NOTES

1. George Gilder, *Wealth and Poverty* (New York: Bantam Books, 1981), pp. 217, 219.

2. Milton and Rose Friedman, *Free to Choose* (New York: Avon, 1980), pp. 48–49, 273.

3. Katsuro Sakoh, "Japanese Economic Success: Industrial Policy or Free Market?" *Cato Journal* 4 (Fall 1984): 537.

4. Sakoh, "Japanese Success."

5. For a detailed discussion of Japanese cultural values and their relation to Japanese economic success, see Johannes Hirschmeir, "The Japanese Spirit of Enterprise, 1967–1970," *Business History Review* 64 (Spring 1970): 13–38.

6. Ezra F. Vogel, *Japan as Number One: Lessons for America* (Cambridge, MA: Harvard University Press, 1979), p. 235.

7. Tom Ashbrook, "Japan Works on Ending Workaholic Ways," reported in *The Eagle,* Bryan/College Station, TX, December 22, 1985, p. 3F. For specific information on weekly hours worked in the years 1960–1985 for Japan and the western countries, see, *U.N. Statistical Yearbook 1983–84,* New York, 1986, pp. 91–92.

8. Jon P. Alston, *The American Samurai: Blending American and Japanese Managerial Practices* (New York: Walter de Gruyter, 1986), p. 4.

9. Alston, *American Samurai,* p. 4.

10. Jon Woronoff, *Japan's Wasted Workers* (Totowa, NJ: Allanheld, Osmun, 1983), pp. 16–18.

11. Data for all years, 1960–85 are not reported in the OECD survey. For consistency and representativeness, wherever possible, data for decade and mid-decade years were selected.

12. Sakoh, "Japanese Success," p. 539.

13. Jon P. Alston, "Japan as Number One? Social Problems of the Next Decades," *Futures* (October 1983): 346.

14. U.S. Department of Commerce, Bureau of the Census, *Statistical Abstract of the United States 1986* (Washington, DC: U.S. Government Printing Office, 1985), p. 24.

15. "Statistics Present Japan as Rich Nation of Poor People," *The Eagle,* Bryan/College Station, TX, November 4, 1987, pp. 1A and 10A.

16. The Oriental Economist, *Japan Economic Yearbook 1981/1982,* Tokyo, pp. 188–89.

17. Robert J. Samuelson, "Our Japan Obession," *Newsweek,* August 12, 1985, p. 56.

18. "Statistics," *The Eagle,* November 4, 1987.

19. Samuelson, "Japan Obession."

20. Thomas A. Chisholm and William C. Schaniel, "The Changing Japanese Consumer: Implications for the United States." Paper presented at the Academy of International Business, Southeast U.S. Region, November 1987.

21. See Norman Gall, "Black Ships are Coming?" *Forbes,* January 31, 1983, pp. 67–71; and U.S. Department of Commerce, *Statistical Abstract, 1986,* p. 190.

22. Organization for Economic Cooperation and Development, *Historical Statistics 1960–1985* (Paris: OECD 1987), p. 83.

23. Jon Woronoff, *Inside Japan, Inc.* (Tokyo: Lotus Press, 1982), pp. 48–49.

24. Japan Economic Journal, *Japan Economic Almanac 1986,* Tokyo, p. 13.

25. Charles J. McMillan, *The Japanese Industrial System* (New York: Walter de Gruyter, 1984), pp. 31–32.

26. Allen D. Manvel, "Taxation and Economic Growth: Another Look," *Tax Notes,* March 17, 1986, p. 1187.

27. Akio Mikuni, "Spend! Spend! Spend!: A Radical Cure for a Constipated Economy," *Intersect* 2 (April 1986): 18.

28. U.S. Department of Commerce, *Statistical Abstract*, p. 321.

29. For corporate tax figures for Japan, See Mikuni, "Spend!" p. 8; for U.S. figures, see U.S. Department of Commerce, *Statistical Abstract 1986*, p. 306.

30. U.S. Dept. of Commerce, *Statistical Abstract* 1986, p. 9.

31. U.S. Department of the Treasury, Internal Revenue Service, 1040 Form, Rules, and Instruction Package, 1987, p. 37.

32. For an in-depth review of Japanese government agency activity in the economy, see Chalmers Johnson, *MITI and the Japanese Miracle: The Growth of Industrial Policy, 1925–1975* (Stanford: Stanford University Press, 1982); Ezra F. Vogel, *Comeback* (New York: Simon & Schuster, 1985), pp. 11–176; Jon Woronoff, *Asia's Miracle Economies* (New York: Sharpe, 1986), pp. 25–67; and Nobutaka Ike, *Japan: The New Superstate* (San Francisco: W. H. Freeman, 1973), pp. 55–108.

33. Vogel, *Comeback*, pp. 64–65.

34. Johnson, *MITI*, p. 235.

35. Ike, *Japan*, p. 61.

36. Chalmers Johnson, *Japan's Public Policy Companies* (Washington, DC: American Enterprises Institute; and Stanford: Hoover Institution, 1978), p. 22.

37. Kenichi Ohmae, *The Mind of the Strategist: The Art of Japanese Business* (New York: McGraw-Hill, 1982), p. 231.

38. Johnson, *Japan's Public Policy Companies*.

39. Vogel, *Japan as Number One*, p. 242.

40. Sakoh, "Japanese Success," p. 537.

41. Richard E. Caves and Masu Uekusa, *Industrial Organization in Japan* (Washington DC: The Brookings Institution, 1976), pp. 16–17.

42. M. Y. Yoshino and Thomas B. Lifson, *The Invisible Link: Japan's Sogo Shosha and the Organization of Trade* (Cambridge, MA: MIT Press, 1986).

43. See, for example, Richard M. Cyert and David C. Mowery, eds., *Technology and Employment: Innovation and Growth in the U.S. Economy* (Washington, DC: National Academy Press, 1987), pp. 24–50.

44. Economic Planning Agency, Japanese Government, *Economic Survey of Japan 1981/1982* (Tokyo: The Japan Times, 1982), p. 239.

45. U.S. Dept. of Commerce, *Statistical Abstract 1986*, p. xxiii.

46. Herbert Stein, "The Economies of American Defense: Q & A," *Wall Street Journal,* July 7, 1981, p. 28.

47. Cyert and Mowery, *Technology*, p. 39.

48. Cyert and Mowery, *Technology*, p. 40.

49. U.S. Office of Management and Budget, 1986, reported in *Newsweek*, March 10, 1986, p. 5.

50. Hal Bowser, "How the Space Race Changed America: An Interview with Walter A. McDougall," *Invention & Technology* 3:2 (Fall 1987): 26.

51. Issac Shapiro, "Second Thoughts about Japan," *Wall Street Journal*, June 5, 1981, p. 24.

52. For a detailed discussion of the role of protective tariffs in the development of U.S. industry, see Frank W. Taussig, *Some Aspects of the Tariff Question* (Cambridge, MA: Harvard University Press, 1915); and Sidney Ratner, *The Tariff in American History* (New York: Van Nostrand, 1972).

8

The Public-Policy Agenda
Reconsidered

The world is a confusing and complicated place, and it is not unreasonable for us to seek to simplify its complexities if we can. There is more information than we can possibly assimilate on more topics than we can possibly keep track of. We face choices and decisions about things we can know only shallowly, if at all. It is natural for us to seek any trusted source of direction amid all this uncertainty and ambiguity.

Political ideologies and organizations supporting these ideologies can become important cue givers and direction providers in seeking to sort out the myriad political choices that face us daily. By accepting a particular ideological perspective and the groups that endorse it, we can be spared many of the difficult examinations and evauations that are needed to make appropriate political choices. This is a very tempting orientation for democratic citizens to embrace, because to reject it, even in part, requires much extra work and thought on our part to sort out appropriate policies.

There are problems, however, if we succumb too much to this temptation. While giving over some of our choices to narrow, ideological cue givers may help us psychologically to sort out some of the complexities of political life, it does not really reduce the actual complexity of the situations we face. The problems remain complicated and difficult, only the solutions are now presented as simple and straightforward. The result of this oversimplification is that we may fail to recognize the true nature of the problems we face and the actual, not ideologically prescribed, actions we will need to take to resolve them.

The preceding chapters have pointed out the ideological positions held by many conservative individuals and groups today and the policy directions emanating from these positions. We have examined conservative assertions about wealth and poverty, the role of government, decentralization, markets, social-welfare programs, and economic success abroad. We have seen that conservative rhetoric on these issues is often more than just an oversimplification of complex phenomena—it is sometimes an obfuscation of countervailing evidence. The conclusion from this examination is that the policy prescriptions growing out of modern U.S. conservative dogma may not offer the best solutions for the actual problems facing our nation.

The real domestic and international problems we face as a nation and as a polity do not lend themselves easily to ideological slogans and simple dogmatic solutions. Our task as citizens in a complicated political environment is to evaluate policy choices as fully and realistically as we can and to pragmatically embrace solutions that offer effective and acceptable alternatives to the actual problems we face. This is a difficult task, but it is one that the American people have historically embraced.

Americans are fundamentally a pragmatic, can-do people. Our history is replete with examples of our avoiding ideological constraints that might prevent us from supporting realistic policies needed to solve real social, economic, and political problems. Whether it was President Eisenhower sending troops to Little Rock or President Nixon visiting China, conservative presidents, too, have generally followed this pragmatic prescription to problem solving.

In many ways, then, the Reagan presidency, with its greater adherence to ideologically based policy making, was attempting a break with past political traditions in U.S. policy making. This is not to imply that that administration was totally ideological or not pragmatic, just that it was much more ideologically oriented than previous administrations. It is my belief that this shift is not appropriate and will not help us address the real problems our nation is now facing and will face in the future. The main reason is that much of the conservative agenda, especially that which addresses problems of social and economic well-being, not only oversimplifies a complex reality but also is based on a very problematic ideological creed.

What many present-day conservatives are asserting about the underlying causes of wealth and poverty and success and failure in our country is a resurrection of a social philosophy advocated by some at an earlier point in our history—a philosophy know as "social Darwinism."[1] What conservative thinkers in this earlier period did, and what has been repeated by conservatives today, is to see social and economic differences among people as the result of a contest between them. Conservatives, then and now, infuse these social and economic struggles with a normative content that implies that the victors, those who achieve greater wealth and position, are in some absolute sense better than or superior to those who do less well in the contests. For many conservatives, then, the contests are mere natural sorting devices that separate those less able, and therefore less meritorious, from their betters. The contests, therefore, are seen not only as necessary, but as having outcomes that are good for society because they guarantee that the more capable win and guide societal events and resources in "better" directions.

This reasoning is seriously flawed. In the conservatives' social-selection contests, like the natural-selection process whose model they borrow, it is the environment that directs and dominates the contest. In social contests, and many natural ones, the environment is not a neutral, unbiased medium. At its best, the environment in natural and social contests is random and arbitrary; at its worst, it is manipulated and controlled. However it is structured, the environment interacts with the characteristics of the contestants in ways that support some and weaken others.

All that can be said about the outcome of such a contest in the natural world of Darwin is that a particular set of environmental circumstances enables one member of a species, with a certain set of characteristics, to propagate better than another member of the same species with a different set of characteristics. It makes no sense, and Darwin would never support the argument that the survivor, the propagator, is better or more deserving than the loser. It is only because of environmental accident that one contestant survives. A different environment, equally random or arbitrary or manipulated, could have worked to the benefit of the other contestant.

Consider the following example. Two variations of one species of frog, one a little more yellow and the other a little more green, have evolved in different but neighboring ponds, separated by a road. Both are doing quite well in their own settings. One day a truck drives by, carrying a particular pesticide to a farm distribution center on the other side of both ponds. The truck has a flat, which causes the driver to lose control, and the truck overturns, spilling out some of the pesticide containers. Several of the containers are punctured in the crash and spill some of the dry chemical into the road. The green frogs are slightly more curious and aggressive than the yellow ones. Several of the green frogs see the spilled material and go to investigate, bringing some of the material back to their pond. The yellow frogs ignore the event. The material that the green frogs bring back to their pond poisons it, and the green-frog population becomes extinct, while the yellow-frog population continues to thrive.

The environment, in this case the random event of the truck accident, has "selected" the yellow frog over the green one. The yellow frogs are not inherently better than the green ones. In fact, many might say that the slightly greater curiosity and courage of the green frogs are superior traits. If the material on the truck had been food, the green frogs might have benefited, but because the material was poison, they suffered. In such a "contest," it makes no sense at all to say that the victor is more deserving, or better. The yellow frog is only luckier, in that its traits were better suited to the environmental situation than were the green frog's.

The same problem exists when some conservatives try to tell us that one group in the social and economic competition is better or more deserving because it achieves more in a given social, political, and economic environment. The environment, either by accident, or more likely because of design, benefits certain competitors' characteristics. Winners often win because the environment favors them, not because of some natural superiority, merit, or worth. The social contest is not some cosmic arbiter of merit, which correctly metes out proper rewards and punishments to competitors. It is, at best, a random and arbitrary process and at worst, a manipulated struggle in which one set of competitors designs an environment that benefits their side in the struggle. In the best-case scenario, the victor is often better positioned to manipulate the environment.

The key point is that it is not any inherent superiority of the more successful competitor, merely the accidental or planned conjunction of certain individual and environmental characteristics, that results in one competitor achieving more or less than the other. We must not make the mistake of assigning worth, merit, justice, or naturalness to the outcomes of such social competitions, especially when the environments are so often manipulated by some of the competitors themselves.

In spite of these serious flaws, however, many conservatives today, President Reagan included, firmly believe that life is a competition and the "losers," the poor and less successful, are there because they lack the meritorious character- istics that have brought others success in the competition. The implicit assumption is that the competition is neutral and fair and that the characteristics found are better in some absolute sense. The logical conclusion is that the victors owe nothing to the losers and that helping the losers is to help inferior characteristics survive, when they should be allowed to become extinct. The conservatives are wrong on all counts: The setting is not neutral, the victors and losers are not necessarily deserving of their fates, the losers' characteristics are not necessarily inferior, and help is not only appropriate, it is necessary.

Mired in these flawed beliefs, some conservatives persist in recommending ideologically based policies to the abandonment of our pragmatic traditions. Policy makers holding these social-Darwinism beliefs seem confident that cutting taxes for the more wealthy and reducing programs for the poor are appropriate policies designed to benefit the deserving and punish the less deserving. They are convinced that spending less for the poor will accomplish more. And they are comforted by conservative scholars who bring them "evidence" to prove that their positions are correct and empirically valid. As we have seen in these chapters, however, such comfort is misleading and inappropriate.

The American public and some leaders of both political parties seem to be reacting more negatively to this increase in the ideological casting of our public policies. For most of our history, certainly our post-World War II experience, the U.S. electorate and the major political parties have been pragmatic and middle-of-the-road. Even in 1980, the year in which Ronald Reagan was first elected president, polls showed that more people supported a hypothetical party of the center than Reagan's Republican Party: Republican Party, 20 percent; Democratic Party, 36 percent; center party, 31 percent; no opinion, 13 percent.[2] Earlier presidential candidates, like Republican Goldwater and Democrat

McGovern, who were to the right or left of this central core, were strongly rejected at the polls. The political parties, while clearly differing in basic philosophies, both sought to remain pragmatic and close to the center. Reagan was the first relatively noncentrist presidential candidate to be successful, and he was anxious to bring his ideological agenda to center stage in the U.S. policy-making process.

Ronald Reagan wanted his administration to be the vanguard of a party and ideological realignment in U.S. politics. As we saw in Chapter 1, he made some headway in the early part of the decade, but the momentum may have stalled. While the electorate remained very supportive of Ronald Reagan the person, and while they may think of themselves as more conservative now, they have not yet fully embraced his ideological agenda for the United States, as shown by recent public-opinion polls and elections. The loss of control of the Senate by Republicans, their failure to gain significant increases in the House, and the failure of candidates close to Reagan in social and political philosophy, particularly Jack Kemp in the Republican presidential primary contests, indicates this weakness. In addition, many recent national and public-opinion surveys show that the public is much less supportive of Reagan's conservative agenda—deregulation, decentralization, military spending, reduced social programs, Contra aid, and tax breaks for the wealthy—than is the president himself.

National and state opinion surveys conducted in late 1987 and early 1988 indicate the public's lack of support for Reagan's ideological agenda. The August 1987 Gallup Poll reported that when asked how best to reduce the deficit, only 21 percent of respondents wanted cuts in social programs, while 58 percent wanted to cut defense spending—just the opposite of the priorities of the president.[3] A January 1988 Gallup Poll asked a national sample of respondents whether they would like the next president to continue Reagan's policies or to change them. Only 34 percent of the respondents wanted to continue Reagan's policies, while 58 percent wanted to change them.[4] Similar questions were asked of 1,000 Texans in the February 1988 Texas Poll. The Texas figures were quite similar to the Gallup ones—only 37 percent of the respondents wanted to continue the Reagan policies, while 55 percent wanted to change them. And the direction of change sought by Texans, as in the national samples, was clear. They wanted to see fewer cuts in social programs and more cuts in defense spending.[5]

Some leaders of the Republican and Democratic parties, too, seem to be more openly rejecting the ideological cast to politics that Reagan has encouraged. Increased bipartisan cooperation on foreign policy, social-welfare policy, and the budget, and a more pragmatic, nonideological approach taken by many of the major candidates in the 1988 presidential nomination process, may be early indications of a return to a more pragmatic American politics and a growing rejection of ideology as the principal director of domestic and foreign policy. The realignment Reagan sought may not come to pass. Political leaders and the public may now be starting to react negatively to his ideological approach.

Movement back to the center may be in the offing, but it is not yet assured.

The weaknesses of the ideological approach pointed out in this book need to be understood and evaluated, and more support for pragmatic, nonideological problem solving needs to be encouraged. We are still in danger of embracing a particular conservative ideology as the oracle of our public policy. This is against our political tradition of compromise and pragmatic problem solving. I do not endorse our tradition merely for tradition's sake. This way of approaching problems has been good for our nation. It has allowed appropriate action and new policies when they were called for to meet changing social, economic, and political needs. The inescapable fact is that ideology is not a sound basis for dynamic, democratic governance.

Ideology and ideologically colored evidence do not lead to good public policies. They do not encourage us to look at the real situations and alternatives that face us, and they do not help us make appropriate and publicly supportable political decisions. Appropriateness and support are important concepts in this discussion. They mean that our policy makers should produce decisions that are in line with our values, which we then can support as a policy. If our officials stray too much from this course, because of ideological self-righteousness or ideological certainty, they may lose sight of the fundamental principles that bind us as a social and political system. Ideological certainty can lead one to play fast and loose with established rules, structures, and conventions. Ideologically supported ends take on a life of their own, independent of our cultural values and legal guideposts. Such ideological certainty can lead decision makers to feel that their ideological end is more important than our system's democratic means. This is dangerous.

Overzealous service of ideological goals can lead not only to inappropriate and ineffective policies but also to the polarization of our society and the subversion of democratic principles themselves, as the Iran–Contra scandal has demonstrated. The conservative ideological agenda of the 1980s has failed to solve either our domestic or international problems, it has left us with an unimaginable debt, and it has threatened the very foundations of our constitutional system. Eight years of ideologically inspired social and economic policies have exacerbated, not improved, social and economic conditions in our country.

One of the real impacts of the Reagan administration and its ideologically conservative allies has been to limit the debate and control the agenda on domestic policy in the United States. Through the skillful presentation and communication of their ideological dogma, they have made positive governmental action on social-welfare policy and economic-development policy seem off limits and inappropriate. It is unfortunate that a flawed ideological perspective, skillfully marketed, has prevented us from successfully addressing the social and economic problems that confront us. We need to return to a more pragmatic, less ideological political agenda, where discussions of the potentially positive role of government in the social-welfare and economic-development areas are no longer taboo. Discussions of these issues need to be returned to the policy agenda and evaluated objectively, not ideologically.

The new, pragmatic, open agenda should include discussions of the realities of poverty and wealth, should be cognizant of the real strengths and weaknesses in markets and government regulation, and should seek, to build on our past successes to facilitate the social, economic, and political advancement of all our citizens. Our nation has not failed, as some conservative ideologues would have us believe. We are in an uncomfortable period of transition—transition in our own economic and social institutions and in relation to our foreign competitors. We have learned much in our pragmatic past to address these problems, however. We do not need to embrace unproven and inappropriate ideological shibboleths.

Our most pressing domestic-policy concerns relate to our social-welfare policy and economic-development policy agendas. These areas require objective discussion and debate. In designing pragmatically based social-welfare policies, we must recognize that much poverty is situationally and environmentally based. Poverty is less the result of bad values and weak survival characteristics than it is the result of negative social, economic, and political environments, leading to lack of skills, lack of opportunity, and lack of the inheritance of human and fiscal capital resources. Government programs, therefore, must have two goals regarding poverty: to try to reduce it overall and to try to soften its impact where reduction is not possible.

To help reduce the incidence of poverty, government at all levels can develop policies that reduce discrimination and that facilitate the development of human and fiscal capital among impoverished groups. This means greater national, state, and local assistance to public elementary, secondary, and higher education. It means greater encouragement of entrepreneurship among disadvantaged groups through loans, executive development assistance, and government contracts. And it means government regulation of negative government and private-sector practices, such as red lining or exclusionary zoning, that discriminate against disadvantaged groups and areas. These policies will not end poverty in the United States, but they may reduce it somewhat, or at least slow its advance.

Our biggest immediate problem is to develop policies that soften the impact of poverty, increase the quality of life of the poor, and give them the real possibility of escaping poverty's grasp. The purposeful neglect and hostility recommended by the conservative ideologues is not sufficient. And depending on general economic advancement alone is not the answer. Cycles of positive, general economic development will help many of the marginally poor escape over the line, but downward cycles will pull many of them back again. And many, especially the hard-core poor, will remain below the line, regardless of short-term economic trends.

It is not creating dependency to assist both these groups. Housing, food, job training, and health-care assistance neither increase nor decrease dependency, as measured by welfare-roll longevity. They do, however, improve the quality of life of poor people, and may even lower long-term costs by nipping chronic health and social problems at earlier, more acute stages. More importantly, these policies of help say something about our nation and its values, which mark our self- and international image as a moral, humane, caring society.

To support such social-welfare policies does not mean that we should spend money foolishly or indiscriminately on any antipoverty scheme that comes along. We cannot and should not support any and all social-welfare efforts, irrespective of their costs, efficiencies, or short- and long-term social and economic consequences. The determination of program worth, however, the determination of the relative merits of governmental and private-sector activity, and the determination of the relative importance of spending money on some programs compared to others, must be based on objective and pragmatic, not ideological, evaluations.

Our future economic development policies require a similarly, objective approach. It is simply unacceptable to assert, on ideological foundations alone, that government has virtually no positive role to play in facilitating economic development in our country—that these decisions must be left primarily to market forces and the private sector. Our history has shown us that both government and the private sector can and do play a role in moving our economy forward. Rather than exclude discussions of each's proper role on ideological grounds, we need to investigate objectively the appropriate role each can play in spurring economic development in our country.

One area where increased government activity may be particularly appropriate is in increased research and development assistance for the commercial sector. Policies that place more R&D resources in nondefense categories, policies that facilitate the transfer of scientific discoveries to the market place more quickly and effectively, policies that better transfer Department of Defense and other federal laboratory, technological, and information-management discoveries to the private sector for commercialization, and policies that encourage interfirm cooperation in R&D and technology transfer need to be evaluated and considered. Such policies are hardly radical; they are tried and proven mechanisms that grow out of our own past experiences and that have been very effective in other nations.

Developing useful and appropriate solutions to the social and economic problems we face as a nation will depend upon our pragmatic approach to these problems and to the solutions available to us to resolve them. It is from this type of objective, empirical, nonideological analysis that we will arrive at solutions that will work and that will be supported by our citizens. It is unhelpful and unwise to reason from broad ideological principles only. We need to return to a more open, more pragmatic, less ideological policy agenda.

NOTES

1. For a very thorough discussion of social Darwinism in the United States, see Richard Hofstadter, *Social Darwinism in American Thought* (Boston: Beacon Press, 1955).

2. Figures reported in the *Gallup Opinion Index,* Report #177, April-May 1980, p. 64.

3. *Gallup Report* #263, August 1987, p. 23.

4. Figures reported in the *Houston Post,* February 19, 1988, p. 1.

5. The Texas Poll is a quarterly survey of Texans' attitudes, conducted by the Public Policy Resources Laboratory at Texas A&M University. The poll results are syndicated in newspapers around the state and are available from the Public Policy Resources Laboratory upon request.

For Further Reading

For those of you interested in getting more information and different perspectives on the issues presented in this book, I can recommend several sources for you to consider. On the general issue of the "culture of poverty," Chiam I. Waxman's *The Stigma of Poverty* and Charles Valentine's *Culture and Poverty* are good places to start. On the specific issue of the tendency for many to blame the poor themselves for their condition, few have presented a better critique of this argument than William Ryan in *Blaming the Victim*. On the issue of the relative success of various ethnic groups in the United States, Stephen Steinberg's *The Ethnic Myth* challenges many of the stereotypes about the causes of success and failure within various immigrant groups.

For two somewhat more ideological discussions of wealth and poverty in the United States and the "proper" roles of government and the private sector, you may want to read George Gilder's *Wealth and Poverty* for the conservative slant, and John Schwarz's *America's Hidden Success* for a more liberal view. A good source of information on the historical trends in U.S. poverty and on government attempts to battle it can be found in James T. Patterson's *America's Struggle Against Poverty 1900–1980*. The important roles government and the private sector have both played in economic development in the United States can be seen in Stuart Bruchey's *The Roots of American Economic Growth 1607–1861*, Louis M. Hacker's *The Course of American Economic Growth and Development*, and W. Elliot Brownlee's *Dynamics of Ascent: A History of the American Economy*, 2d ed.

Two good sources of information on the nature of economic growth in Japan and Japanese business practices are Chalmers Johnson's *MITI and the Japanese Miracle* and Jon Alston's *The American Samurai*. A great deal of useful statistical and descriptive information about Japan can be found in the various *Economic Survey of Japan* books published by the Japan Times, Ltd.

Index

ability, monetary accomplishment and, 42

achievement. *See* success

advantage, inheritance of, 55–60

advertising, market economy and, 90

Advisory Commission on Intergovernmental Relations, 68

advocacy groups, myths and, 10

age, job skills and, 120. *See also* elderly

agriculture, government support of, 98–99

AIDS research, 101

Aid to Families with Dependent Children (AFDC) program, 113, 121–25, 127

American Indians. *See* Native Americans

American Journal of Sociology, 22

Ashenfelter, Orley, 119, 120

assets, familial transmission of, 56–57

attitudes, defined, 55

aviation industry, government role in, 99

Banfield, Edward, 19, 20–25, 34

behavior: rewards for, 54; standards for, 55

beliefs: traditional, 3; types of, 55

Bellah, R. N., 8

Bell Laboratory, 100

Bernstein, Basil, 25

blacks: attitude barriers for, 49–53; education and, 72–73; environment of, 44; geographical distribution of, 48; government programs for, 26; handicaps of, 27; human-capital development and, 48–49; income of, 46; legal barriers for, 48–49; material wealth of, 41; presidential prospects for, 52; quality of life, 44; self-concept of, 53–55; in single-parent families, 35–37; South and, 60–61; success and, 26; violence and, 61; voting and, 71–72; West Indian immigrants vs., 27–34; white attitudes towards, 43, 44, 49–53

Bogardus, Emory, 49

British Journal of Sociology, 25

Brittain, John, 56, 57, 58

Bureau of Standards, 100

Campbell, Angus, 43

cancer-drug development, government role in, 101

capital: economic growth and, 139–40;

ABOUT THE AUTHOR

ARNOLD VEDLITZ is Professor of Political Science and Assistant to the President at Texas A&M University. He received his Ph.D. in Political Science from the University of Houston in 1975. During 1980–81 Dr. Vedlitz was on leave from Texas A&M, serving as an analyst with the Office of Service Delivery Assessment in the U.S. Department of Health and Human Services. In this capacity he acted as a principal or coprincipal investigator on nationwide evaluations of Department of Health and Human Services programs. He has published widely in the areas of American political behavior, minority politics, and urban politics. He is the author or coauthor of articles that have appeared in the *American Political Science Review*, the *American Journal of Political Science*, the *Journal of Politics, Social Science Quarterly, Urban Affairs Quarterly, Sociological Spectrum, Economic Development Quarterly, Annals of the American Academy of Political and Social Science*, the *Journal of Black Studies, the Journal of Negro Education*, the *Western Journal of Black Studies*, and other journals.